50p

To Colin

OTHER TIMES

with Love
bjitl

By

Gilly Cowan

• • •
i

For all those who had to endure and then survive life having witnessed the full horrors that mankind is capable of inflicting on itself.

Only for hunger would an animal, unprovoked, be so barbaric to another animal.

Dedicated to my mother, Dorothea, Mappen, Eddie – IKZDZ, Peter and Heidi, my children and my grandchildren.

Chapter One

Since starting the research for this book I have had some restless nights, since the feelings of my dead mother, my brother who still lives in Germany, as well as my own little family, had to be taken into consideration. We - my mother, my brother and I - had to live through all sorts of troubled times, just as did many more people who came from the East. There is no scope for settlement down here on Earth as long as many countries do not see eye to eye. Human beings can only live in peace if and when they are prepared to accept that they are all different. Any political ideal is dangerous for the human race as it includes an ideological system which is elevated to dogma. Whoever is taken in by it is completely lost, to the world around them and to themselves. Very often the world stands in flames following one of these beliefs.

It is far more profitable to recognize a pretender, because blame and reconciliation are not inseparable. One has to beg forgiveness, as do others. We cannot dig up the innocent bodies, but their fear and sufferings should be a lesson to us all. It is virtuous to forgive, but this does not mean that one has to forget or be resigned, but rather that one should encourage the togetherness of people. Through war, escape, deportation, expulsion and pursuit in various ways, about 16 million Germans were resettled from East and South Europe. 1.9 million were from Pomerania alone. 800,000 of the Pomeranian population lost their lives. That is 26.4% of the total population. It took until 1964 to clear 90% of all queries to do with the loss of the Eastern Sector.

Nothing is more irresponsible than to suppress the truth, even if it is not to the liking of the Germans, Poles, Russians, British,

French, Americans or Japanese. It is necessary to report as far as possible the whole truth of what happened to the civilian population in the East, even if the figures on both sides do not tally. It is quite shocking to think that the hunting down and destruction of human lives became a social pursuit.

The Devil appears to have more volunteers than the Lord. It leaves to us the task of choosing between the helpers and the missionaries, since we all had Hell on Earth enough in the war period, so deep was the grief in my generation. There is an urgent need to start again. Whoever wants peace should draw a very thick line under everything and start a new paragraph. To shift the blame from side to side is hopeless. War does not always solve problems, it sometimes creates them.

Rudyard Kipling once wrote;
If any question why we died, tell them, because our fathers lied.

My family; that is my mother, my brother and I, lived in a small town in Prussia called Schivelbein, now Swidwin. My mother was born there, as was Peter, my brother. Apart from Stettin, now Sczecin, where she went to the conservatorium for her music studies, she lived there for more or less all her life. My grandfather was Director at the Technical College in the town. He was born in Pyritz, now Pyrzyce, which was another little town in Pomerania. He was well loved by us all and taught us our first letters and sums during the occupation. He certainly was a well respected personality in the small community. Swidwin was at that time still a country town. When my parents married, they moved for a short time to Regenwalde, now Resko, where I was born in 1938.

Sunday, 12th May 1985.
I am now entering a stage of my life where a lot of things could go topsy-turvy.

❀ ❀ ❀

4

It is a very cold morning, the wind is blowing around the corners and anybody would have to think twice about putting their feet onto the cold floor. After 40 years and a lot of travel, to go and see where you came from is quite a shock. Shock in so much as you need the courage to face up to the future. The future often lies in what we have come through as children. The memory of long days and nights can haunt us. We can only hope this is not translated into doubts, fears or anticipations of the time ahead. After a good continental breakfast with lots of hot coffee and little conversation, our minds are full of thoughts of the future and past. It sounds melodramatic, but to take a journey back to the past and stay in the present is not something which happens every day to you.

The bus leaves at 7pm from the bus terminal. The City of Lübeck has the sleepy stillness of a Sunday morning. Quite a few people have arrived at the meeting place and are talking in excited voices. Most of our fellow passengers are older folk and have taken this trip before and going by their country style clothing, belong to farming estates. We, my aunt called Mappen and I, are taking the journey to the place where I was born. Lübeck is a city of 224,000 inhabitants. It is a very old harbour town, otherwise known in German as a "Hansecity". It was founded in 1138 on the little river of Trave, which runs into the Baltic Sea. This city accepted us 39 years ago as refugees from the East, not quite with open arms, but nevertheless it took us, fed us and clothed us to a certain degree. I spent most of my younger years here. Lübeck was, and still is today, a very proud city. It had an influx of 90,000 refugees after the war and has today the distinction of being the only city along the border with East Germany. Its beautiful Cathedral was bombed on the 29 March 1942 and with it a fifth of the old town. Today, Lübeck is again a symbol, the well known silhouette for those entering into West Germany from the Baltic Sea - a homecoming very few people can ever forget. Thirty-nine years ago it certainly seemed to us like Heaven with peaceful days and nights ahead.

Our first hurdle now is the border crossing of Schlutup-Selmsdorf. Schlutup is today as it was 30 years ago, where we as schoolchildren played in its forests, climbed the trees and sprang over its bogs. The restaurant is now in ruins; the ice cream was never any good anyway. But if you listen hard enough you can still hear the laughter of the children echo through the thick woodlands. If you translate mood into words, then you might say that this forest changes my own dark foreboding into silent whispers of what I do not know. At 8am the crossing opens, that is to say the customs men will be ready to frighten the unsuspecting travellers out of their wits. Borders can be crossed anywhere in the world, but none is as overpowering as this one. On the Western side no problems. The usual intent of people on long journeys is to find the toilets, since we are not allowed to stop along the route in East Germany, except at the allocated points. We wait one and a half hours in anticipation. All our faces fitted to passports, a performance repeated, it seems, ad infinitum. The DDR soldiers then drift away not to come back for a long time. Waiting is always long, but when you have a British passport amongst a busload of German passport-holders you grow restless.

It gives us a peculiar feeling to think, that it is now 39 years since we crossed this border, but from the other side. Also at that time there was no official border; it had not been clearly defined. It was on 6th April 1946 that we came to Künitz, a suburb of Lübeck. We were then put into barracks constructed from corrugated iron and ate from metal plates that could have done with a good clean, but we were happy to have food and to be alive. Six people were allocated to one mattress. After that, began the, by now, usual process of de-lousing with showers and powder. The smell hung around for days. It was a gruesome place; children were crying a lot, dying of malnutrition and other diseases; women looked old and haggard, the strain of their long and desperate journeys showing on their faces. Yet somehow they were also glad to have reached the West, as it was called even then. But little did they know that they were no more welcome here than in the East. The only comfort they could draw from all their misery was that at least they were still in Germany.

We went from here to the next place of rest, the "Bunker", an old air-raid shelter, now converted to house the refugees from the Eastern parts of Germany. Even then we were Poles and Russians in some people`s eyes. But as in every war, everyone looks after themselves. So did, at that time, the German Red Cross. They presented us with soup, from which the potatoes and meat had already been taken by the helpers, who seemed to get fatter by the day, while here every day someone died, since the meals were issued for a certain number of people per day. The dead were still included so as not to reduce the amount of food sent to our bunker. The cream for the Red Cross helpers was therefore more abundant. After all the hard times and struggles to get to the West, then to die just seemed unbelievable. But then every war has its innocents to pay the bill. After a short spell, however, a kindergarten was opened and the children were fed better and escaped the horrors of that bunker for some time. Soon after that, the schools were restarted. Luckily our grandfather had taught us during the time of Polish and Russian occupation in Pomerania, so that my brother and I could go to the school and be taken into the classes appropriate for our ages.

My first impression of the new school, the Dom First School, was not the best. It boiled down to the announcement by the teacher: "Poles sit at the back". I did not move, since I did not feel spoken to, but she then pointed to me and there was no mistaking whom she meant. A slap on the fingers and I was soon moved backwards. It was quite a frightening experience for a girl of seven years of age to be treated by her own people as if she was scum, or often as if she did not exist. Someone to trample on, someone who should do tricks and dance on command. When it came to Christmas and money was collected for the poor, my teacher was disgusted that I refused to give. We simply had nothing to give: we were still on the clothing list ourselves. My mother had not even received her widow's pension, since my father was killed near the Crimea in 1942. At least we did not lose out on our schooling, but we hated every minute of it. The reminder, that we were not proper Germans came in many small and large comments. This was taken to the extent that we were not allowed to use the toilets with the other pupils. We had to wait until last.

Shortly after that we moved to a new "Refugee Camp", Finkenstraße, where we had our own room. Fairly soon we built our own bed from planks and straw. At least it was off the floor, but being wood and straw it was an attraction for fleas, lice and any other bugs and a constant battlefield with those little beasties. My mother placed little metal plates under each bed leg with a foul smelling disinfectant to keep the little creepers in check. Some months later furniture arrived from my grandfather and aunt. Both were separated from us and moved straight from the bunker to Jever in Friesland. My aunt took up her old occupation as dressmaker, since the people there had not really felt the war too hard and were able to afford new clothes. It was a farming community and food came easier, and, with that, money as well. From then on and for many more years the British Officers wives were well-paying customers. The British Camp was not too big and one wife had to be seen to be better dressed than the other. My grandfather was receiving his pension, to us more of a miracle, but it paid for our beds. We also got a cooker which ran on coal and gave us heat, a table with inserted washbowls, chairs, and a wardrobe. We were rich, or so it seemed. The wardrobe was empty of clothes, but that did not bother us. After months of orange boxes and blankets we had a palace and a place to cook properly, whatever food came our way. We guarded these new found riches with vigour.

Unfortunately, soon afterwards my mother developed angina pectoris and was transported from hospital to hospital. It was a very hard and unsettling time. Very often for two young children, 9 and 7 years old by now, a very long trek. My mother's bedding had to be taken wherever she went and not by ambulance. Since none of our relations lived in Lübeck, we bundled it together and carried it there. Bedding, nightclothes and toiletries were certainly not supplied. I learned very soon to steal wherever I could; survival was the motto. Not until many years had gone by did I realise that stealing was not the done thing. It seemed to belong to the order of the day. Nobody ever told me different, bar my mother. Everybody just nodded and said: "good girl". Mind you I only stole food.

Under our room was the only place where we could store food stuff, so we dug a large hole, the soil around sealing it from any predator we thought. The little rats thought otherwise and tried to steal our potatoes. We made it our game to sit with our catapults or stones and shoot at our visitors as soon as they started their squeaking. After a while even they got the message and stayed away, so our struggle on the fields picking potatoes was not in vain. Our vigilante force had been an unqualified success. It had however cost many sleepless nights and endless supplies of small and large stones. Also a very good aim was necessary. Practice makes perfect. Now I feel very sorry for my mother, for the commotion she had to endure, since she was still not well. But then food was by far more important than a night's sleep, for that we had years to catch up on. Along with the potatoes we also picked endless turnips. A meal which I cannot face to this day. At that time, however, it was our staple diet and we were grateful for it.

There is a certain peaceful feeling when going to bed without squeaking coming from beneath the floorboards. A certain feeling of well being made you fall asleep faster and deeper. A day in the fields picking potatoes or turnips is quite back-breaking, even for children, but we had to be busier than my mother so she would not have to go back to hospital. It felt like losing all security when she was not there. We loved her very dearly and thought that with our stealing we did a good job for her. Now I shudder at the thought and know what she must have felt when we brought more food home and she had no idea how it was acquired.

My mother had been out of the hospital for a while and our next project was a shed. Looking back, it was such a comical construction. At the time it was very serious work and tremendous thought went into it. Without a hammer or nails, how to make such a structure? Simple - with string, of course! Oh yes, and it withstood all sorts of weather, storms, other people and us two children. To the three of us, our achievement was out of this world. We had a shed! We could store our collected wood and padlock it, as we found a working padlock with a key in the undergrowth of the nearby forest. My mother soaked it in soapy water and spared a drop of our cooking oil for it. The cooking oil of that time was fish oil and smelled and tasted absolutely terrible. It did the job, however, for our new treasure, the security lock.

For a mother with two children, a girl forever in trouble for being on the lookout for food and a boy not even old enough to look after himself, we must have been more than a handful. But somehow it did not seem that way, we took every day as it came. Others had, after a while, a father who came back from the concentration camp, but we hadn`t. Therefore someone had to look for tomorrow's meal. My mother's pension had by now come through and there was at least some money to buy goods with. Even to queue for carrot bread and other food articles was a part of our daily routine. One of us would queue at one shop and the others somewhere different and so we brought sometimes more than one loaf home. More often than not this happened between 4 and 7am in the morning. School started at 8am and we had a long way to walk to reach it. In the very cold winter of 1947 I received my first new coat. It was made from a white blanket and scratched terribly. It looked like a bell tent, but since I was tall and skinny it was a marvel and very warm. On a long and cold day in December I had my first attempt at home sewing. From a dark blanket, without a sewing machine, and with inferior thread I produced a pair of trousers for Peter. They actually looked quite reasonable, but when looked at closer, how could they have? I had no idea about sewing. I sometimes wish I could show part of our life to my children. Maybe they would not even believe me. Even I find it often hard to swallow. In spite of all the shortcomings we had a beautiful close relationship with my mother and friends in the same boat and did not seem to miss a lot. Play came in the evenings, when we all had the daily tasks behind us. We made our own dolls from rags, and dressed them. We used orange boxes as beds for them. Played with the boys "Kippels". A slightly sharpened four inch long stick, which you hit with another stick similar to cricket bat. Hide and seek was a well tried game, since it did not need any material. Skipping, hopscotch and all sorts of guessing games passed our time.

One day in a crowded tram, right in front of me, a lady left the tram and left two bags standing on the floor. She had obviously come from a visit to a farm. She took four bags with her, how she could have carried the others? I shudder to think. I moved next to the bags as if they were mine, waited for six stops and finally left the tram with my newfound treasures. I had to walk nigh on four miles back with this heavy load. Six stops were a long way, since it was on the greenbelt side of Lübeck. My poor mother nearly had a heart attack when she saw what I had found. Flour, eggs coffee, sugar and lots more. She would not use any for a considerable time, but then she was grateful for the food. We often thought of the woman and thanked her with all our hearts. It helped us to survive, we hoped she did not miss it too much. The pension my mother received for the death of my father was very small and lasted for a fortnight instead of a month. Our efforts to grow carrots and other vegetables were not successful. The Australians must have found what we put into the ground, since we did not. Out of our window we could see lots of appealing fruits including apples, pears and plums. These were to be found in allotments tended very lovingly by their occupants who were often very hard in their attitudes. For a long time we were the intruders and did not deserve anything, since it was we who had lost the war. Even worse, we had started the war. It is quite amazing how twisted some people's minds work. To children with hunger in their stomachs all this was water off a duck's back. We got a long stick, put a nail in it, and with this instrument we fished the fruit out. Some gardeners were more understanding and left full baskets just behind the fences. Needless to say, we looked after these gardens and were very polite to these people. Others left containers so we could fill them for the owners, our reward being that we were allowed to pick all the fallen fruit for ourselves. Sometimes we had some fruit left after our own use and sold or exchanged them for other goods.

It was a hard school to go through to survive, therefore making us appreciate more what we have today.

To bring us back to our journey, very close to the border there is a great wall that runs along the "Lübecker Bay". At more or less regular intervals are the lookout towers with their roving eyes. Not even 5km distant is the first road block. DDR soldiers are ready to check our passports and faces again, as if the border police have not done their job. We are now entering a no-man's-land. Even today we find that the people living here have to ask permission to have visitors from the West or even their own DDR sectors. Stopping is only permitted at allocated places. When, however, it comes to the Mark (the German equivalent of the pound before the Euro) you can change and spend as much as you like. All this we are told as we continue on our journey. Although everyone wants one Germany, no one is prepared to give a little. The East is East and so educated, while the West is afraid of all the spies that may come across.

We are on the 105 now until we reach the Polish border. On one side is still the Bay of Lübeck and of course the Wall, but why around the water? We are passing Bassow, a small country town. Very nice, tidy kitchen gardens and front gardens. A sleepy little place. Very large banners are on display for the end of a war 40 years ago. "YOUR BIG BROTHER IS WATCHING", "WHAT WE HAVE ACHIEVED, WE ARE GOING TO KEEP" or "ONLY WITH OUR BIG BROTHER CAN WE LIVE IN PEACE". It is hard to understand that such an amount of propaganda can actually be produced. They seem to have taken the Third Reich's advice in producing enough propaganda and with that make the population actually believe in it. So, what had the last war achieved if now the same tactics were again in use? The USSR can be proud of such a large following, considering that all of these people have suffered under their earlier regime. How quickly the memories are blocked out and new times take over! Further and further we travel through lush forestry and sandy, hilly countryside to Gravesmühlen, with its beautiful town gate into the little town, but then it transforms into grey blocks of flats. The people here don't seem to laugh; they are tidy and smartly dressed, but grim faced and with hanging heads. If any of the population of Mecklenburg were evacuated after the war, I do not know. I found no evidence. Obviously they did see the suffering, since thousands of refugees must have crossed their territory. Brandenburg and Saxony must have been deeply engulfed in the refugees moving back to Pomerania and East Prussia.

These refugees had already seen the war from every other direction and were then turned back by the Americans to their "Homeland". Brandenburg and Saxony were lying more on the way of the now dividing German border and were used as a buffer. The troops from Great Britain and America must have had a hard time, but then they only went to Berlin.

The route we are now taking brings us through lovely clean, wide sweeping, agricultural areas. There are beautiful little lakes nestled in fields and forests, but with no one in sight that might fish or even walk along their shores; but then, it may be too early. There are, however, the first people on their way to church. We now enter Wismar, which was, being a harbour town, 60% destroyed during the war. Today there are Russian ships in the harbour, Russian and DDR soldiers walking more or less side by side. Wismar is now one of the military encampments of the DDR. Many of its streets have still the cobblestones as known to us from the pre-war period. Everything is still very quiet. As a centrepiece in the marketplace there is a large tank war memorial. A little beyond Wismar, is a large lake with boats and a camping area. Quite a few people are sitting fishing here. The earlier comment was too soon about nobody to be seen. A spot for silent minds. In Bad Oberon we have a very old Spa town with left-over old villas in reasonable repair. Not many cars are to be seen on the roads, as in the whole of the DDR so far. A small strip of flat road unfortunately ends too soon. And again, there are not many free places where propaganda for the Remembrance Day is missing. From here, we soon enter the important harbour and military stronghold of Rostock, also an old Hansetown, trading-place to Denmark and Lübeck. Again Russian ships are resting peacefully against the pier. The town itself has a tramcar and dual carriageway; one has to be a little more careful not to get under the wheels now, though there is still no comparison to the traffic in the West. We have now reached the official stop and we can actually stretch our legs and have some coffee. The town has been rebuilt in the old style and looks quite lovely. It is still very cold outside and few people are moving about on this gloomy May Sunday. Children are playing around the bus. They are waiting for their chocolates, for every bus which stops here obviously has sweets for them. Quite a few of our travel companions started shortly after Schlutup with their breakfast and have munched ever since. Could these people be afraid that someone would take their precious food from them? Or are they thinking that what they have eaten nobody can take? Nervous energy consumes a lot of food, and these people don't know what they will find at "home" as they still call it.

On the 108 the journey continues to Lage, surrounded by the most elegant carpet of fields in blossom. The colours are varied, from the brightest yellow to glowing red and bluebell blue, shining in the sun, which is just pushing some rays through the clouds. From Lage to Teterow it is not a great distance. The little town well known through motor-racing. Between the Kummerower and Malchiner Lakes on the 104 forward we go towards Malching. Even the roads overland are in a shocking state. The villages and little settlements look lovely in colours of fresh paint. The only spoiling effects are the continual displays of propaganda. The streets are at the moment being cleaned and trimmed for the Peace Cycle Race which takes in the whole of the DDR, Poland and Russia. We reach Neu Brandenburg, a town upon which the Second World War has taken its toll. Here is a charming old city gate with large archway, into town. Composed mainly of large barrack-type houses, grey and broad. Some of the old houses and estates are well kept, including a well preserved mill fully overgrown with ivy. The 104 seems to go on and on. In its path lies the small market town of Woldegk, where now the market sports flower beds and tubs and, of course, red flags. In Prenzlau, the province town on the edge of the Unter-Jecker-Lake, are moored sailing boats on which the owners seem to be awake, and a colourful camping site encircles the calm waters. Himmler made Prenzlau his headquarters. After him, it was occupied by Field Marshall Heinrici. For Himmler it was a place to be far away from the fighting on the Eastern front. Heinrici, however, wanted to be with his troops and by that time the front had moved in that direction. Heinrici received his orders to be Commander of the "Heeresgruppe Weichsel" towards the end of the war, when Himmler could no longer master the stress of war. Heinrici was the son of a parson and worked his way up the military ladder. He had command of the 4th Army in the Eastern battlefields. He was very much living in the present and able to keep the obtainable and unobtainable in military men and equipment apart. He was an officer brought up in the Prussian school and so indoctrinated with Prussian honour. But more about that later.

Now at long last near Pomellen-Kolbtizow is the Polish border. We have to fill out a customs declaration stating all our money, jewels, cameras and any other goods of value that we are carrying. Then comes the same procedure as at the DDR crossing, faces, passports, luggage and one and a half hours later we are on our way again. As usual when we have navigated some difficulty, people have to relieve their anxiety by spending, this time in the Intershop. However, it does not take long. Nervousness sets into these pilgrims, who are getting restless and starting to shuffle about. The roads or motorways are very uneven, in parts wider than the roads in the DDR. Everything looks untidy here, where the motorway is coming to a sudden end. Now we are in Pomerania, the part of Germany that was fully German before the Second World War and only after 1945 transferred to the Poles. So far, however, there is no peace treaty signed. East Pomerania and Silesia, plus Gdansk fell together under that regime, while East Prussia and Memelland came to Russia. Sudetes and Bohemia became independent. Our limbs are starting to get stiff, while our eyes have taken on a slightly glazed look.

Stettin, now Szczecin, Pomerania's old capitol, lies with its large cranes and harbour installations to our left. Across the River Oder we are now on the transit route from Szczecin to Gdansk. Alongside a beauty spot we have a short coffee rest to the concert of croaking frogs. Thousands of the little creatures are settled in this swamp called the "Buch-Moorlands". Bees, other insects and flying objects are buzzing around our heads. It is a very sticky and swampy area. Delicious fields and rising hills now break up the landscape on both sides. I cannot remember when I saw my last stork, but one now looks majestic as it sits on the tower of the next church. The nest is extremely large and does not appear to be the most stable of constructions, but what a sight! We are told that 3000 pairs still nest here every year, produce new families and then set off to more temperate climates.

I was always under the impression that all rolling stock of the pre-war railways had been destroyed, but no, we have just seen one. Mind you, how the people can see where they are going is beyond me. The windows are caked with filth.

One of the forests, visited by West Germans every year, the Prutt Forest, lies on both sides of the way. Huntsmen are allowed to hunt here every year, at a price, of course. This is a very peaceful part of the country with the Burgermoors on our left. We are now reaching the area where the fields and agricultural lands run into each other, interspersed with marshland and boggy patches. Enormous fields in yellow and green unroll themselves before us. The houses and barns are all in need of a coat of paint, or even cement, as most of them are actually in need of rebuilding. These materials, cement and paint, are not to be found here. If anyone has visitors from the West and they can bring these goods with them, they are the rich ones. Very often these goods are sold by the Poles for colossal sums of money. It seems that time has stood still here.

The fields are just about to come into blossom with the yellow and green hops. To frame it all, there are the most beautiful roads with trees growing over the roads to touch like an archway. It is a journey into the "Green", quite romantic and relaxing.

Next comes the little town of Gollnow, now Goleniow, from the old Golinoz, translated as "in the middle of the forest". Well known for the gothic Wolliner Archway, which is 26m high and one of the largest town gates in Pomerania. It is a sign that Goleniow was once an important harbour and trading-place. It even belonged in the Middle Ages to the "Hanse", a rich merchants' association. At that time, however, only small ships went up the Inna to unload and reload with timber, corn and salt. The town is encircled by old "Wiekhouses", with all their towers and gates. After the clearing of the war, only remnants of the Powder and Coin Tower and the Wollinger Gate were left. St. Catherine's church from the Middle Ages was rebuilt 1957-1959, but otherwise the Old Town was left in a sorry state. The rebuilding here was done in a very simple style, very much in contrast to the old picture. Square housing-blocks now form the town centre and the old Mansion house was never rebuilt. The market is cold and forlorn. Inhabitants number about 28,000. North of Goleniow lies the airport for Szczecin. From 1945-1975 Goleniow was the seat of the Polish district magistrate, within whose region was the old Naugard, now Nowogard, and Southcammin district, including some communities from the Satziger region. This helped, of course, to increase the population of the town which was 60% destroyed. After Goleniow, which is really a town of many children, dirty, untidy streets and washing at most windows, our journey continues via Barfußdorf, now Zolwia Bloc, through an idyllic pasture. The fields spread further, the forests are much thicker, sweeping hills more rolling and even. The green seems to be far greener than in the West. Maybe imagination is playing a trick, but it does look a very rich green and almost all the occupants on the bus comment on it.

Now we reach Nowogard, lying on a mostly dirty and overgrown lake with just a hint of rowing boats. Nowogard was once a quiet district capital, the rural surroundings comprising two groups, the Scots pines on the one side and the Gollinger moorlands on the other. In the east, however, lies the open "Druminlandschaft". Sorry, there is no translation available for this word. The land was formed through the Ice Age. Surrounding Nowogard with its dips, trenches and lakes. The Wallenhills (Osen), run from North-North-West to South-South-West; the country blooms. The small town was formed on the point of the "New Citadel". Even in 1274 it was known as "Citadel and Market Place Nowogard". It became, through a gift in 1248 to the Bishop of Cammin, "Naugard and the Land Naugarde", and from then until 1945 was in the hands of the Dukes of Pomerania. 60% was destroyed in 1945, nearly the whole of the old town part. The western part by the lake was still not rebuilt. The centre of the market is taken up by a monstrous statue (TO THE BROTHERS IN ARMS). The town mansion was saved. To its right stands the new district house, also a hotel since 1975. Today there are about 12,000 inhabitants.

Next along the route lies the tiny town of Plathe, now Polty. It nestles directly on the cross roads to Szczecin, Köslin, now Koszalin, Kolberg, now Kolobrzeg, and Stargart, now Targard. Before the war this was a little agricultural community and therefore without defence. It was named Medina in 1277, and for hundreds of years was in the possession of the "von der Osten family" with short spells in between belonging to the "von Blüchers". These were Pomeranian titled noblemen. In 1904 the new gothic town church was built and is still a monument this day. The von Osten and the von Blücher castles are also still in use. The von Blücher castle was destroyed by fire in 1866 and, rebuilt by the Poles, now houses the "Dependence of the Szczecin Archives" plus the rest of the "Bismark Ostenden Library". Until plundered by the Russians in 1945, it contained priceless documents of Pomeranian history.

The post road through Pomerania to Gdansk, accepted as being old, even in the Middle Ages, was often used by armies, as in the Seven Year War. The Russians used it often as quarters, as in 1945, when 65% lay in ruins. Even Napoleon rested his troops here. The sunshine has finally come through and lays its rays across this land. The small farmhouses, most of them dilapidated, seem to shine in its sparkle. The larger estates in Poland receive Government assistance for agricultural machinery etc. However, much of the work is still done in the fields with pickaxe and plough. Horses do their job in pulling the plough, while peasants collect the stones which are thrown out, or lay the potatoes by hand in the furrows. So far we have come across a good number of fowl and pigs. Now we see, from an old and run-down scrapyard, that the West has arrived. Even our Western scrap-merchants, domiciles look like palaces against this scene. Everything is so ramshackle and dirty.

We are nearing the end of our day. The road winds its way through green low hill sides, forests and marshlands with wide open pasturelands and fields. We see the vision of a large carpet with all the colours of nature, only broken through nature's design. Very few tractors or cars appear here. One has a distinct feeling of not being concerned about being run over. At the junction of the rivers Persante and Radue lies alluringly, on a small elevation in the corner of the rivers, Körlin, now Karlino, overpowered by its late gothic Michael's church. This old market town once had a large castle which was taken over by the Bishop of Cammin in the 14/15 century. Because of its position Karlino has seen a lot of hardship in its history. In 1945, therefore, the damage which was inflicted was no exception. Even today it is a typical Pomeranian town with about 5,000 inhabitants.

My father was here for a time. He worked at that time in his life for an insurance corporation; he also helped out on a farm at harvest time and promptly lost his wedding ring in the hay. After leaving school with the equivalent of "O" level, he had gone into apprenticeship as a car mechanic, and having passed his exam he then enrolled at an agricultural college (Stadtdomäne Hoffmann) near Stargard to take an apprenticeship and after that a diploma in farming. He had a good and strict teacher and passed his exam. To make all this into something lasting he had to serve at various estates for a time as an inspector, until he went for a year to help his brother Karl in Wilhelmstal near Beustettin. 1934 was the time to sell the small estate and my father enlisted in the "NSDAP" later to become SA leader. By this time he was well into insurance, run by my paternal grandfather. It was not his natural occupation at all, but as grandfather Kratz disapproved of the Nazi Party, he had no option. During the Röhm affair (May 1934) my father was badly beaten up and also accused of being associated with SA leader Peter von Heydebreck, who was a homosexual. This was very much forbidden at that time. The beating left my father deaf on the left ear and he also suffered dizzy spells thereafter. His innocence was later proved, von Heydebreck being shot shortly afterwards. To prove oneself innocent was, under the Hitler regime, a difficult and costly affair. It cost grandfather a packet, but then this was the only cost he ever had for his youngest son. Once proved innocent it was wiped from the slate. From 1938 my father was forbidden to enter his family home because of the connections to the Nazi Party. Grandfather Kratz was a staunch opponent of the Party, he was an old Royalist and an officer and very proud of it.

My father was stationed in the Nazi training camp near

Swidwin and met my mother at a dance in town. The family was not too pleased when she brought him home, since grandfather Hoppe also had his own ideas about the activities of the Party. However, everything seemed to have worked out alright, since they got married on the 14th of May 1937. After that they moved to Regenwalde where I was born in June 1938. My father enlisted at the beginning of the war and was posted with the 23rd Tank Division as sergeant and officer in reserve to France. Here he met up with his twin brother, who was stationed in Paris. Apparently they had a good time there. Subsequently, in April/May 1942, the twins went with the 23rd to take part in the retaking of Charkow in the Ukraine, but the attempt failed. My father's tank was blown sky high. All that was found and given to Hally, my father's twin brother who was a doctor, a few days later, was one finger with his second wedding ring. Earlier, Hally who was stationed near Charkow decided that it was time to visit his brother. The Division Commander thought he was seeing a ghost, since both brothers looked identical. He was, however, sent from one brigade to another, before someone told him that his brother had been killed the day before. We received later a death certificate from the Wehrmacht, so my mother could claim a pension, which never amounted to much.

Back to the journey. Before Koszalin stands a monster of a statue, a very large potato cupped in a hand- a mark for the potato land, which we found out later to be appropriate and wondered even more why the potatoes we were served at Milldams were so horrible or did we only get the grey looking ones. In Koszalin itself it looked as if time had stood still since the war. It now has many new housing estates, but still a lot of rubble and ruins. Here are grey blocks of concrete, on the lines of military barracks only higher, and the by now usual "flags" of washing in every window. This, however, gives the buildings a touch of colour. The footpaths are literally potholes, impossible to negotiate in any type of shoe. The buses are crammed to the last centimetre; the doors have to be forced close.

Our "first class" hotel, Jalta, is a case for the Trade Descriptions Act, a grey block of mostly dirty windows and filthy curtains. The entrance hall has a very worn, threadbare carpet. One has to be careful not to trip over all the fringes. The staircase is without light; the landings have a most pungent smell; 157, our "suite", complete with bathroom and shower, has a ghastly smell. First activity is to open one of the windows, but only one will actually move and do us the honour, only to be nearly falling out. So we have to block it open with a folded newspaper. The table is a real beauty, so rocky not even a cup will stand on it without sliding sideways. The armchair is good to look at, but not to sit on. The arms just fall off. The wardrobe, however, is of the latest design and with modern tricks. There is no key, no handle to open it with; this has to be achieved with a hard bang which then reveals one solitary bent wire coat-hanger. Luxury at its best! After the struggle comes an interruption with shrieks from the bathroom. My aunt went to the bathroom to flush the toilet, hoping some of the smell would vanish, but, oh dear! - the whole canister came apart. She has the handle in one hand and the lid in the other, while water splashes everywhere. It than takes the maid nearly one hour to come and have a look and put it together again. So, even emergencies are slow to be resolved. The smell, however, of course remained.

The washbasin is so large that two hands fitted into it and that was that. The best still is that the swivel arm is longer than the basin, so you get very wet feet every time you have a wash. With a jiggle of the water arm the water will just run into a corner of the basin, if you are very careful, that is. Cleansing materials seem to be missing altogether, or the cleaning woman has a holiday every day. We are nonetheless well served, since the rest of the travellers are using the loos on the landings which are completely blocked. Towels and hand towels are like washboards, hard, stiff and very grey. So we now use one of our kitchen towels and a guest towel which we had brought with us. Both were to be used in the bus after our meals. This was to last for four days. How we just creased with laughter!

As usual there is a way out of all sorts of predicaments if you try hard enough. The smell was terrible in the place, even opening the window did not help. There was so little time before dinner to clean yourself, including teeth. The bottle with mouthwash fell on the partly tiled floor in the bathroom and broke into many pieces. What a beautiful aroma, what a most gorgeous smell, what a relief! We inhaled it with full lungs. At last our room was habitable. The clean, fresh air stayed for all of our four days there. It was a wonderful relief when you had to walk through the corridors and then come into our room. At last we arrived for the reception banquet in an unfriendly dining-room whose curtains looked like dishcloths that could have done with a really good wash and starch. Nestling behind these creations were some ominous black boxes. The purpose of these was not specified. The music did not come from them, but wires running into the walls did. The crockery was out of this world, extremely large cups, the size of two cupped hands; the coffee pot was so large that one had to stand up to lift it; all was of a very heavy stone material. The cutlery was of very light metal with, believe or not, white rust! It is unbelievable that these things can actually still be used. This hotel is in regular use by tourists coming to visit their old homesteads. The meal itself was very primitive: potato puree, grey meat - nobody could guess what kind it was - and six pieces of cucumber with a white sauce. If there was a desert, I can't remember it. As a drink we had a pinkish sweet lemonade, it was to be our staple drink on this journey. Our table was very inconvenient, as we all had to get up if one wished to get in or out. Of course, we were also blessed with the "dear old Ladies", who seem to appear on all of these trips. Two particular "madams" were sitting to our right on the bus. They slept most of the way, and for the rest, they ate. Nothing, however, was to their liking. They were always the last wherever we went, a complete nuisance, but very important to themselves.

The question of transport for the next day arose. Could our two dear matrons come with us in our taxi, which so far we had not even booked? That would have been the last straw. Across from us sat an old couple, where he did exactly as he was told. His speed in speech made it difficult to understand him, which meant that one inevitably gave the wrong answer. Both ate as if there was no tomorrow, and that it was their last meal on earth. The second couple was younger. He was from Schleswig-Holstein (a province in North Germany), and no mistaking. They are a jolly, phlegmatic breed with mostly large frames and a broad "Pladdeutsch" to boot. A proper farmer, who had all the anecdotes that come with his occupation. He had us in stitches. But soon tiredness kept conversation down to a minimum.

After the meal came the task of finding a taxi-driver for the next day, since we wanted to go to Kolobrzeg and on Wednesday to Resco and Swidwin. I was told there would be difficulties in finding the right person who could speak German, but we had no trouble whatsoever, as the receptionist had one waiting. We agreed a reasonable price, in DM of course, and a pick up time.

We took a quick stroll along the High Street to stretch our legs and view the very sparse shop windows with inferior materials on display. At the end of this crumbling road lay a gorgeous park, with precisely groomed trees, clean benches and a very clear river flowing through. All very restful to the eye, and quiet after the hustle and bustle of the day. With a slight breeze playing in the trees it was relaxing to sit and watch the world go by.

Just one beer and into bed. Our bones were not speaking to us anymore. The bed itself was hysterical. The cover was so lumpy, heavy, grey and damp, that one had the feeling of a wash house atmosphere. Mappen at least had a proper bed, while mine was a three-part couch with many more bulges than a straight bed. Over hills and deep valleys was that night's sleep. Mappen's lamp was fastened with a paper clip into the back of the radio. It sparked, but gave no light. The wires just hung down. What a day!!

Monday the 13th May 1985.
What things, tales and adventures will cross our path today?

Breakfast at 9am. After the enormous washing procedure in our mini-basin and the bone-shaking exercise to reach some semblance of a living body, we march down into the dining room. Apart from tea, the rest was quite adequate, with homemade gooseberry jam (very appetizing) and bricks for bread rolls, as well as ham pate. At bus time you would think our travellers have a seat to catch the way they were all pushing, but we all have our seat numbers. Some of course are late. Our guide is ready to show us HIS country as he calls it. We picked him up at the border yesterday, since no bus is allowed to travel alone.

The weather has improved and even tries to let the sun peep through. Today we are scheduled to visit Groß Mölln, now Mielno, and Koszalin itself.

Koszalin was established in 1226, later became Hansestadt and lies at the foot of the Gollenberg, now Chelmo Slawienskie. Before the war it was a cultural and educational centre with all the essential offices of North-Eastern Pomerania. From 1815 it was an administrative area embracing ten rural districts and three town districts. Its circular-shaped old town was an example of thirteenth century earth settlements. Before 1945 it had about 34.000 inhabitants; now it has over 100.000. The Red Army caused tremendous fire damage in 1945. Because of an increase of outlying areas the land extent has increased to a current 17.994 sq km. The Polish government moved into the old government offices which were damaged. The northern side of the market received a new town hall. The Marienkirche was rebuilt and has been since 1972 a cathedral with 174 parishes.

The town itself was extensively rebuilt with an inner ring road from the station to the Gollenberg through the Miller's Gate suburbs in a big bend to the Gobacher Street, past a settlement for 20.000 people. Of course, enlargement brings with it the farm people moving into town and the neglect of the agricultural land.

The Main Street is dreary and unfriendly. The old government offices are still in use but desperately need a fresh coat of paint. The Marienkirche normally holds musical evenings, but at the moment only the bells ring at night. In spite of the settlement for the Poles there are very long waiting lists for statehouses or flats. Their cost is very high. It is said there are more millionaires in Poland today than in the rest of Europe. They just have no opportunity to spend their money. On the whole this is a bleak town, since nothing has been rebuilt in the old style or any pleasant form.

We leave Koszalin on the old "Danziger Street" (now "Street of the Red Army") in the direction of Gollen (Golin). The road leads direct to the 137m high and clearly visible elevation - Homehill of the Koszalin population - the Gollenberg with its Gollencross. This was erected in 1829 in memory of the Liberation War.

After Napoleon had marched twice through the stricken city

and devastated it even more, the cross was thought to be a reminder of that time. The cross is beautifully worked in wrought iron and stands proud and tall between the lush green trees of the forest. It could do with some paint, but on the whole is a beautiful sight. As far as we can make out only visited by old expatriates.

Soft leaves cover the ground which on one side fall very steeply. The park is today, as then, the property of the town. Along the forest edge the road continues to Kluss now Klos) and joins with the new motorway from Gohr. What was at one time a Sunday Park is nowadays a wilderness with no walkers and so far not even animals. Thousands of people used to come and worship and admire the cross, but today the footpaths are slippery and the mixed forest is not tended. The restaurant has only broken windows and its roof is gradually blowing away. It is, however, surprising that the Poles have left the cross, since it is a German monument; everything else German has been destroyed. Our guide tells us that the history of Pomerania began only when the Poles moved in 1945. What a pity! It must have been a beautiful and restful place.

Our next destination is Zanow, now Sianow, where three of our ladies disembark. A very small place, it even now has the not falsified character of old Pomerania. It was known before 1945 as the "Matchstick" town, as it had a very large matchstick factory lying in the old part of the castle. The people of Sianow were also known to be extremely forthright.

We smell sea air, for Laase, now Lazy, lying between the Baltic Sea and Jarmunder (Jamno) Lake, is now on the horizon. Here for the first time are some old "Sommerwege", lanes which have one side sand and the other side gravel. Depending on the time of year one uses one side of the road or the other. Surprising, but they are obviously still in use.

Today they are covering the lanes with tarmac. After that we go on to Deep, now Czajcze, where nowadays the army has large camps from which everyone is kept away. The little village is overrun with soldiers. Next comes Groß Mölln, one of a hundred Pomeranian holiday resorts on the Baltic coast.

No other German county has so many resorts as Pomerania. It would take too long to name them all. On this protracted coast and its half peninsula, enriched with numerous bays, the sea sweeps along the steep coastline and produces its shifting dunes. Along the coast with its lush pastures and deep Scots-pine forests lie fishing villages which are used as lovely holiday resorts for inland people, as far away as Berlin. In a way it is not surprising that West Germany would like these parts back. The sea and its beaches are a wonderful sight and West Germany is short on coastal areas.

The Jamno Lake, a lovely lake, with campsites and mixed greenery around it ,which seems to be quite deep enough for boating and diving. Mielno is today one of the sea resorts for government-run hospital and convalescent homes for the working population. Very few people are on the beach. The beach itself is beautifully white and soft. I have, of course, tried the Baltic waters with my feet. The water is quite clean, bluish and very cold. Many of our compatriots are now old people and don't think that they will see these shores again. One lady would like the sand from here be put into her coffin when she goes one day. For that reason we find a few of them collecting sand in plastic bags to take with them. One has to remember, that these people are still very attached to their homeland. Especially since most are old people.

A woman in her forties stopped us. She had heard German voices and told us that she was German and had been left behind after the war to marry a Pole. He was now dead and she travels to the West, but does not wish to live there. She was on holiday. She could not collect her pension in the West, she said, so spends her time travelling through Poland. She has learned to live with all the earlier oppression and fear and now has a reasonable life. She felt accepted now.

For holidays this is a cheerless place, except for its beautiful church, the tower being 57m high. Here again is to be found a vast number of storks and their nests. Unfortunately, this was one of the war areas and the large estates were burned down or bombed or have become so dilapidated it is unbelievable. Very few are actually in use. If it is a large estate, a few families often share it and also receive government funds for it. These estates are and were very extensive and still appear very idyllic. Very often they contain little ponds or lakes. Some of our bus people are coming back tomorrow, since they have recognised their old places and hope to see more.

Some of our travellers look perfectly at home on these farm-estates; the way they hold themselves, speak or even dress is quite characteristic of people native to these lovely fields of hops and corn. This is not meant in scorn; they just seem to harmonise. The older couple on our table are an example, both dressed in dark, long, warm, browny-black clothes. Then we have a gentleman, who could have been a landowner, with his companion, who by the way runs a very respectable girls' school in West Germany. Others are like little animals, which have been away from the lair, dressed accordingly. Some have brought children, now also grown up. These latter families have, however, the look of townspeople now. If, however, one takes the wife of our Schleswig-Holstein fellow, she is still today dressed in folk costume and it suits her in the country she is now visiting. The earth around here looks very wet and moorish, coming up to Funkenhagen, now Ganski, where the old lighthouse has stood since long before the war with its 1300 watts per lamp. It is one of 19 lighthouses along the Baltic coast to Gdansk. The lighthouse is in good condition and in a marvellous setting of fields in blossom. The road to it, however, is very, very narrow and marshy. Nine lighthouses near Gdansk and six here show the seafarer his way home.

Right in front of us is the inventor's dream, a matchbox bus, a box on wheels with a cab hung on the front - a school bus no doubt with all the laughing children facing us from the inside. It looks very funny, but I doubt if I should want to ride in it. The suspension does not work or is even installed, since the children bounce up and down when driving through all the potholes or bumps in the road. But as children I don't suppose they notice it at all. Whatever it is they are having fun. On route to the village of Jamno appear the first potato fields, not long sown since the plants are still very small. The hops, however, seem to get brighter in colour every day. It leaves the countryside with a beautiful bright yellow sheen.

The route from Koszalin to here is not really for buses, since the roads are extremely narrow and winding. All villages with the old ending of -hagen in their name were once upon a time rich villages with their wealthy owners of large estates. Jamno is today, and has been for generations, a very affluent place. At the organ, in its beautiful old church, is still today (and so far the only sign of anything German) an inscription in German that the confirmation class of 1922-23 collected to have the organ restored or repaired.

Along charming forests, fields and meadow-tracks we make our way back to Koszalin. On the way lies one of Europe's largest paper mills. After the First World War, with shortages of wool, the paper produced here was used for knitting. A little further on is a very large fruit plantation under Government control, also a giant flour-mill and factory, coupled with a corn-utilisation plant. Both are also under Government control, of course. The fruit trees here are all of the low, bushy variety and full of flowers. All these factories and research centres are supposed to produce better food and also the new-style farmer. With all the research and planting it is amazing that no better and varied food is served.

Shortly after that comes an old riding-school, where before the war princes and nobles were instructed in riding. Today it is a large leisure centre, badly in need of paint and restoration. Fences would not be a bad idea, since the children would be protected from the traffic on this reasonably busy road.

We have reached the enormous houses and their washing-lines again. There is no washing at all in the courtyards or gardens. A wide road brings us back to Koszalin to the spot where two roads run into one. On one arm lies the main post-office, while the other side has the market and a shooting-gallery. Further on is the old station from where even today the "old Fatty" (alter Klüter), as the train is known, still runs to Bublitz (Boboliz).

What a busy morning it has been! At last a rest and dinner-time to unscramble one's thoughts. The culinary delights are not too fantastic. On the whole it is a very nice meal. Everyone seems to be in their own private world. Good or bad thoughts, that is difficult to say, since this group is so very different in character.

The afternoon is spent with our taxi-driver and his son. The son (22 years old) is supposed to take over the business in a year or two, but still has a lot of German to learn, so father says. It is amazing how many German people who once lived here come back every year. It will always be their Fatherland and of course their birthplace. It also shows the amount of money there is in Germany, to be able to afford these trips so often. The Poles have learned how to charge by now, also to boost the currency market with asking for DM instead of Sloties. These tours themselves are very expensive and the accommodations are very often very poor.

First of all we follow part of the road we took this morning; then via Barth, Alt Timmenhagen (Tymien) on our way to Kolberg, now Kolobrzeg. The journey is pleasant and entertaining and, as we are in a Mercedes, very quiet - lovely! The whole area gives you an easy relaxed feeling, but it does not stir the feeling of a homeland or Fatherland in me.

Kolobrzed, the Salt City of the East, saw some of the worst fighting and was about 90% destroyed. Whoever knew Kolobrzeg in its old glory, visualises its old beauty and the magnificent cathedral. The cathedral was a very distinctive landmark known all over Pomerania, looking and with its large bells sounding out into the Baltic. With the town, which was long fought over, the cathedral, a brick building, with its colossal mass shaped by glazed stone and blind corners, fell into ruins on the 8th March 1945. All the beautiful ceiling paintings and other precious relics were lost forever.

In 1254, one year before the German colony was imposed on the city, the old Marienkirche (Church of St.Mary) was declared useless. Shortly after that, the new Marienkirche, now cathedral, was built. The old church was most likely in the old town. The first service was held in 1282. In 1316 money was collected again to enlarge it further. The building of the high choir was finished in 1331. From the original three-storied church hall a pentahedral building was formed by adding two aisles by the end of the 14th century. The old framework of the roof stayed. In this way the nave was broader than long, 40m broad and 22m long. Increasing only by the massive tower construction, it received the stamp of approval as a genuine piece of Pomeranian culture and craft.

On the west side were two towers, 42m in height, which had to be held together by a connecting building. The last building on the north tower was completed about 1430, each tower having added to it a low pyramid roof; the connecting building, however, just a stone-built roof, 14m high, in 1646. A powerful foundation was necessary to support the weight of the tower mass. It runs for some metres under the neighbouring houses and stands on the pile work of many thousands of posts.

The unusually large area of the high-gabled church roof was originally covered in wooden tiles which were exchanged in 1450 for copper plates. The slate roofing of the towers was replaced by copper in 1552 and again in 1714. The inside of the cathedral was exceptionally impressive and stunning in its decorations, where many of the people, including the nobility of Pomerania, prayed for hundreds of years and laid their dead to rest; one is overcome by a feeling of everlasting peace even today.

Eight solid, eight-cornered, painted columns hold the cruciform vault of the nave, bending slightly outwards at the top, however, because of movement of the foundations. Behind the altar, resting on six Bornholm chalkstone posts, stands the wooden screen, the only one in Pomerania, dividing nave from choir.

From the cruciform vault of the nave the sun shines beautifully on the 14th century paintings, portraying the life of Jesus and scenes from the Old Testament, the only examples of medieval fresco paintings in German buildings of gothic style. 32 main, 40 side scenes show a beautiful use of space. A very large part had to be renewed after destruction in the 18th and 19th centuries.

One of the best-known copper artefacts in Northern Germany is the famous seven-armed candlestick, a copy of the one in Jerusalem. It was four metres high and was completed in 1327. Three arms were replaced in wood following bomb damage by the Russians in the Seven Years War. Old gravestones stand along the walls of the outer church. From the side arms of the former alderman's seat (14th century) the wooden-carved emperor, bishop, crusader and Virgin look down. On the remaining six oak panels of the choir stall are engravings with flower ending tails, depicting the areas of Pomerania.

Under the vault of the nave hangs the gilded "Schieffenkreuz" (a cross), carved in wood in 1523, one of the priceless and most fantastic church ornaments. Krüger's "Pomeranian History" maintains that there is not another one or its like for beauty.

Worthy of further record are the "Holkenkrone" (Holken came from Lübeck to Kolberg), the copper christening-font, two originals of the older Cranach (an artistic main door-knob), and the exceptionally harmonious organ. Max Gregor, the noted German organist and composer played here. High up in the towers, past the forest of rafters, were the bells. Three chiming bells were housed in the North Tower, the oldest dating possibly from 1272. The Middle Tower had the silver bell and the time bells (the hour bell from 1388). Miles away and out at sea these bells could be heard.

Forever memorable was the outlook from the little chambers in the towers. Not every Kolberger has had the pleasure, whoever has will have a memory of the sight of Kolobrzeg and the Baltic until they die.

8th March 1945 saw the cathedral sink into ruins. Now the roofs of both towers and middle point have disappeared, as well as the saddle roof of the nave. The church was burnt out;

everything; only the sidewalls stood. For two years the Poles built and built, but gave it up again. The massive tower-like structure still overlooks the ruins and rubble of a town sinking into ashes. No bells ring any more from their great height to send greetings to the uncountable German graves spread around the devastated countryside. This information is taken from the paper "Pommern 1952" by Dr.H.Behr.

The cathedral was completely burnt out, but is today rebuilt mostly in its original style. The christening-font, the candelabra and a picture of the last supper were saved. The pillars on the right-hand side are all leaning badly.

More about Kolobrzeg: En route is a 4-star hotel built with insurance money. A vast collection of convalescent homes is to be seen. Kolobrzeg is today a holiday resort for the workers. Before the last war it was a high-class modern Holiday spa. There is a new open-air theatre where every year singers and singing groups from all over Poland meet and compete. The pier has been newly concreted. On today's stormy sea one observes the Polish Navy at manoeuvres. The harbour is at present mainly used for military purposes; very few excursions are made for pleasure trips on the Baltic.

The sand along the beaches is beautifully white and soft. Why can't our beaches be like that? It is very cold and windy, but then it is only just May.

The old grammar school was left standing and is today again in use as school. The Poles care for and restore the memorials not only to the best of their ability, but also to their original style where possible. But they then take on a different meaning, nothing remotely German as they were originally. In contrast we find very plain offices and government buildings, industrial installations and again splendid party palaces for their Socialistic future, but these bombastic buildings can be seen all over Europe in other states.

Kolobrzeg was founded in the 13th century by merchants from Lübeck, Niedersachsen and Greifswald. Two cities in Pomerania were traditionally fortresses, namely Stralsund and Kolobrzeg. Three times during the Seven Years War the Russians tried to destroy the citadel of Kolobrzeg. The battle in 1806-1807 with the Commander Gneisenau and the Citizen Force Commander Nettlebeck against the French is recorded in the history books. The last sacrifice was recently in 1945, when the Red Army encircled the town. Around 90.000 people lost their lives then. 90% of all the buildings were devastated. It literally sank to its knees on the morning of the 8th May 1945.

During the 19th century Kolobrzeg was elevated to the dignity of Spa, mainly by establishing rail links to Bialograd in 1859, by transformation of the salt works into saltwater baths in 1860 and by the removal of the fortress-like installations in 1873. So it changed from a Hanse-Citadel to being a Spa-town. First class swimming facilities and versatile healing processes gave it an excellent name. With approximately 700.000 bed-and-breakfast houses and 58.000 paying guests it was one of Germany's top Spas in 1938.

Along the beach, about halfway between the pier and the harbour, stands the new Hotel Balyth, in place of the once famous Beach Hotel. The complex also takes in the replacement of the Münchner Fort with a lighthouse. Today's visitor also finds a colossal monument, erected to commemorate "The marriage of Poland with the sea". 18th March 1946 was a more or less ritual date for Poles:" We swear never to leave you again, because you, the sea, have been since time immemorial Polish". However, research shows that "Polane means a fieldworker in its true form and so the Poles are inland people"; whereas "Pomeranis are sea people and so fishermen". The name Pomerania was completely erased from all maps in 1945 and registered by the Poles as "original Polish ground".

The new style Kolobrzeg, so very different from the old architecture, is mainly to be found in the town centre and here mainly around the cathedral. Since 1972 the old Collegiate St. Marienkirche is known as cathedral. After the massive destruction of 1945 and a long interim use as a military museum (in the tower and then as a half church in the choir steps were taken, after ceding the building to the Catholic Church in 1972, to rebuild the church. It took much patience and hard work and millions of Sloties to achieve anything. Even today it shows how the foundations suffered from having all the leaning pillars. The cathedral   of Kolobrzeg was one of the Protestant "Minsters" in the northern hemisphere, with its medieval structure preserved.,

Except for the mansion, Home Museum, Powder Tower and the Catholic Church, no house remained standing of the old city centre. This is replaced now by up to 15-storey high-rise flats. Not even from the look-out of the cathedral tower can one oversee these monstrosities and the view is now boring in its monotony. The well maintained sea spa and Hanse-City, after its Bishopric-Hanse type history and citadel tradition, has gone forever. One leaves Kolobrzeg with extremely mixed feelings.

En route from Kolobrzeg to Biolograd, that is directly at the halfway crossing, lies the little town of Karlino. We stop here at a folk-lore restaurant. Our driver and his father are very enthusiastic about the place. It is very pleasant, but also very primitive with wooden seats and a few cushions. The coffee is excellent, only served in glasses here and you could burn your fingers with ease. On the second floor is the bar with stuffed sheep as bar-stools - very novel. One gets the impression that the Poles are not building for the future; everything is done in destructible wood or unfinished concrete. All this grey makes a town, city or place look very unpleasant. The variety is missing and with that the changing of the seasons, where new flowers or trees could produce different colours.

The weather is now starting to play up. It is getting quite dark: the uninviting sounds of thunder are heard and the flashes of lightning show on the horizon, but we have only completed half of our afternoon plan.

So our journey proceeds to Biologard. This old market town was left nearly in peace. Most of the old buildings are standing although in desperate need of repair. The church on the market corner is, like all Polish churches, in tip-top condition. They are just rehearsing for the first communion. It is closely packed with people and flowers. The Post Office directly opposite the church corner must have had a recent coat of paint, it looks very smart. All the little streets have cobblestones. For a large town it gives you the impression of a lovely little village; only the pond is missing.

It is rapidly getting darker and the rain is falling quite heavily, so our return is rather speedy. In front of the hotel, is as a goodbye for today, a very nice heavy shower awaiting us. Since we are a little late, we rush straight in to dinner. I can only remember that we had very appetizing fish with the now usual potatoes and cucumber slices. After dinner everyone had to report from their afternoon out.

The old couple had not been allowed on to their old farm estate. On his parents' homestead they were literally chased away. They could not believe that having come all this way, they would be treated like that, considering that for years they had sent food and clothing to the present owners. Today they had also brought clothes and coffee etc, for the occupiers, which in all the upset they left behind at the farm. The hate of some Poles is even today very strong. It is often difficult to understand the older German generation, since many of them, even nowadays, believe it was Hitler alone who caused all the trouble and not themselves. In fact, one is very often told that they never knew about the atrocities that occurred at the beginning of the Second World War in other countries under German occupation. But that is where the good old Hitler propaganda came in. Propaganda in as much that the country had to be pure, cleaned of impurities. That foreign workers were not allowed to learn or even go to school. The "Masterbreed" was the important thing.

The younger couple had more success. They even got coffee and cake and were generally satisfied with their reception. I wonder what we can expect on Wednesday?
Dead tired we climb to our comfortable suite. After wrapping Mappens' leg into some medicinal liquid, which seems to be a nightly procedure, we got to bed. That is, we first took all the old covers out of the covers and refilled it with a blanket. The duvet was a picture for posterity; no one would give that to their dog to sleep on. Filthy and in tatters as they were, we just could not believe how, so far anyway, a nation could be so dirty.

The church bells from the Marienkirche and the singers, who had already looked too deep into a bottle, were in constant competition. Drunks seemed to be part of the daily life. Vodka seems to be pretty cheap here, and of course, their "Champagne". So ends our second day.

Tuesday 14th May 1985.
This is a day on which a lot has happened to my family in the past. My parents married in 1937 in Swidwin and tragically my father was killed near Charkow in the Ukraine in 1942 on their 5th Wedding Anniversary. My grandmother also died on that date, just as my family received the telegram with news of my father's death. That I happen to be on this day near the place where I was born, I have to thank Mappen, my aunt. I always

wanted to come back here, but without her it would have been a lost cause.

Our destination today is the "Pomeranian Swiss". The harsh country between Haff, Baltic and the Pomeranian lakes is the ideal holiday area and one of the important agricultural sectors of Germany. It's magnificent seaside resorts along the far-stretched coastline and the wonders of nature of Pomeranian Switzerland provided a goal here for Sunday outings for the townspeople, especially those from Berlin.

Our trip begins in glorious weather at 9 am, on the 160 via Klamin, Goldbeck (Glodowa) towards Boboloce, a beautiful stretch of road with moor land, lush trees along the road and some very thick forests. The murmur of the trees is today, however, subdued, since there is no wind. One can't see enough of the beauty of this country, as long as one does not think of and look at the farms spread thinly over the land. Since the improvement of the weather some farmers have taken the opportunity to fertilize the ground with farm manure using forks and spades which makes the smell last even longer. One cannot miss being in a farming area.

The little village of Manow (Manowo), now 600 years old, nestles in an idyllic setting in the Manowo hills.

Kilometre upon kilometre of forest lie along both sides of the road. All of this is now under the National Trust. Along the River Radue we reach a beautiful reservoir (Rossnow is its old name, but I know no translation for this) where in days gone by one could pick the blackberries along the edge from a boat. Today it is a holiday resort, complete with observation points and a repair area for cars, but no more blackberries, or small rowing boats with children. We looked very hard. What an association! Do these cars only reach the next beauty spot repair area? Very often we find beauty and the beast put together. The Hohenzollern-Sigmaringen were the owners of "Gut Rossnow". My great-uncle was manager of the estate and the family was always invited when the owners came twice a year for the hunting season. The great occasion was always the harvest festival, with dancing, cabaret or farce and lots of fun for young and old alike. The "von Kameke family comes from this area. She was a Jewess and did a great deal for her people on the estate, even helping Hitler in order to ensure nothing happened to her or her underlings. Herr von Kameke opened a potato plantation in Schleswig-Holstein after the war. The potatoes are well known in Germany.

Hermann Göring was forestmaster for sometime in the Koppelberger forest. Many people were enlisted to do "emergency work" here. They had to fell tress, cut them into logs and load and unload as required. Graves were at that time not dug in this area, since when anyone got near to dropping dead, they were shipped off to West or East Prussia. There they had to dig trenches; even women and children were enlisted, often just to fall into the pits themselves from exhaustion, illness or literally death. Many thousands died in those counties digging for their country.

Mappen had also been sent to West Prussia to dig for Victory, but since she had an important business to run she was sent home after three months. She had a dressmaking attillie. My mother did not dig because she had a small family, but therefore she had to take in workers from the Ukraine. These people were very good to us children and helped tremendously with the house work, they also very often brought some food home from the farms where they worked.

Near Old Griebnitz we find a vast amount of corn and potatoes, part of the old granary of Germany. The ground is very brown and often sandy. The "Hotel Groß", a well known hotel in this area, can provide anecdotes of Peter von Heiderich, who seemed to have lived his fairly short life to the full.

As 60% of all agriculture in Poland is registered as state owned, 10% only is in private hands, the remaining 30% present us with a mystery. So far there are not many pigs to be seen, but masses of geese, chickens, ducks and pheasants, and, for large animals, cows and horses. Geese and ducks are one of the exports to Europe, coal being the other.

The highest hill in the Pomeranian Ridge is 260m above sea-level. Land drainage goes to the Virchower-Lake. Many large estates worked this land before the war. Nowadays one finds mostly huge potato plantations worked by more than one family, or even sometimes state owned and worked by the employers.

As with most town-centres, Griebnitz has its market-place with its old and proud merchant houses, the church and mansion house. All are in coloured brick and look therefore still pristine, except for their dirty windows.

60% of Bodolice was destroyed. The 26th February 1945 saw Bodolice as a large field of fire. The vast masses of the Red Army came and ransacked, raped, killed and generally had their fun. They poured petrol into the houses and lit up. Many people died in their own burning homes. If anyone wanted to escape, they were driven back into the flames. Often women were just shot if they refused or struggled against giving their bodies to the soldiers, and those were the lucky ones. After the houses were razed to the ground, some people were still found alive in the cellars. In every corner of the town, in all streets and alleyways, there were groups of sobbing and hysterical human beings huddled together. The boots of the soldiers soon drove those people into hiding elsewhere.

Vegetable factories, fruit farms and a wool industry are now here in evidence.

The area of Neustettin (now Szczecinek) is rich in forests and lakes. The town was built in 1310, as a border bulwark against Poland. The deep-lying Streutziger Lake was enriched by the beautiful parks and quiet places around the edge of the water, so much so that Szczecinek was known as the "Pearl" of Pomerania, the town between water and forest. The Vil-Lake lies enchanted and untouched. Before 1945 a lovely restaurant was to be found on the "Mouse Island". The town has today 40.000 inhabitants. It did not see the devastation of property in 1945 and has therefore still its small and narrow streets with their cobblestones and old shops. Benches are pleasantly scattered along the lake edge. Everything looks tidy for a change. The rowing - club and the boat-house, however, scream for paint and/ or new boats.

Furniture factories, woodwork shops and an electrical installations industry have found a home here. For the summer there is a grand sports centre; camping and holiday camps in great variety are to be found. The large brickwork firms produce the most modern shapes of brick, roundish and curved and wavy, probably for building uneven houses. What a disorganised country! At the moment they are constructing an open-air theatre for the Ten Towns Festival which will be held at Whitsun.

After some waiting we are shown the Marienkirche. 20.000 Catholics worship here. According to the priest the church is far too small. The church stands in the shadow of some very old trees. The windows are in old coloured glass and they even look clean. They are delightful to look at, especially when the sun shines through. The church is refreshingly cool, certainly when one comes from the heat outside. It is really a most gorgeous summer's day today, and therefore the church is a pleasant place to rest for a while. Magnificent old paintings decorate the walls of the church which was built in 1310 in the Gothic style.

It has a tower of 78m high.

Next to the church is the parsonage and priests' seminary. In front of this admirable building is the main street and behind it a little brook. Charming flower beds and benches contribute to the whole picture. Largely hidden in trees and houses lies the museum which at the moment is not ready to receive visitors. Szczecinek has also a small church on the other side of town and hopes to build a third one soon. 90% of the inhabitants are Catholics. Looking at the people outside who seem to be followed by dozens of children, one does then feel that the need of more churches is appropriate. It is only amazing when one looks at the houses which are by far more in need of repair and paint. In the suburbs along the lake the houses have mostly been very grand at one time. Even now, ramshackle though they are, they make an impressive picture. It is a pity that the enchanting park like gardens are so overgrown.

The town hall was built by architect Schinkel, in Gothic style, in 1852. The windows are very black with dirt; even a harsh rainstorm could not produce the wonder of cleaning power. The long-standing Nicolei Tower is for the time being the museum.

And now, as with most tourists, all our travellers are so far dispersed, that none can be found. Lunch has been postponed twice. It should have been held in the Hotel "Pomansky". After a rest at the lakeside, where it was extremely delightful to sit in the sun with a light breeze, we are off to be fed. Lunch with soup, main course and appetizing fruit for afters, is really tasty, a great improvement on our hotel. For drinks, however, we have that bubbly, pinkish, horribly sweet water. The restaurant is pleasantly cool and we are all refreshed, so much so that this band of satisfied people are then let loose on the unsuspecting population. First, however, the toilets. This little task gets more unbelievable as regards hygiene than one could imagine. It is ghastly; this time there is not even water for flushing or washing of hands. No one was prepared for all this dirt and the "Cologne" handkerchiefs are fast running out. We have used now as many as one normally uses in a year, and we are only half way through our journey.

Szczecinek used to be the most important town in the area of the Pomeranian mountain range. The town was in the hands of Pomerania for centuries. It was, because of its convenient location on the old trading road from Kolobrzeg to Posen, now Posnan, a bulwark against Poland. In the 19th century it developed into an important rail-link point. The five lines spread from here in all directions. The area is not quite as mobile now.

In the year 1933 large fortifications were built here to hold Poland off. Women, children, men of all ages, soldiers sent for recuperation, all had to dig, and for what? All was worked in a sombre and expectant mood, with fear and trepidation creeping into their hearts. Twelve years after that and the cruel exercise was for nothing; the destruction was complete.

Only twelve years after Hitler took over power in Germany, the Soviets stood between Schneidemühl (Pila) and Kulm (Kulmo). The rail link was built in 1877-78. The building of the troop training station at Groß Born, now Borne, in the 1930's made Szczecinek   the supply centre for this the largest military establishment in Germany. In the course of the last war 35% of Borne was destroyed.

On the 26th June 1945; in the "Pearl" of Pomerania's cities chaos broke loose. Previously there had been no murder or killing of any kind, the town had spent and lived its own life. The population had to die in masses now. Mainly women, children and older people were affected by the march into their town of armies, very often Mongolian. These seemed to be the first troops to harass the women, raping them in hordes. The lucky ones died soon, the others being used again and again. Many women suffered mentally and physically from their ordeals long after the war had finished. Very often women were raped in front their children and other relatives. It was to be a spectacle. Ten to twenty soldiers to one woman or girl was the norm. Some women got around this situation very cleverly by offering themselves to only one soldier and he came back night after night. At least these people were saved to a certain degree from the mass mauling and often murder. Unfortunately the German population turned against them and they lived a life of hatred from their own people; for many it got too bad and they killed themselves.

Three hundred lives were lost immediately after the Soviets entered the town. Most were shot purely because they were in the way; others were dragged behind horses until they were dead. The last deed seemed to be a favoured past time of the Russians.

On 26th February 1945, Shukow, the Russian commander, started his offensive into Pomerania near Szczecinek, and, with that, the evil broke out over the land. In a band of 40k width, Shukow's army wheeled its way towards Kolobrzeg, breaking the thin lines of the 2nd German Army and the 3rd German Tank Corps and so separating the two armies. The tank division blew up every fourth tank so that the others could have their fuel. Each tank had only ten shells left in any case. Shukow's success was soon to be seen and felt. German soldiers reported that from the hand grenades they had, only every fifth one worked. It was always a priority to get the SS out of harm's way, since Himmler was now their full-time commander. Any other parts of the fighting units did not really matter to him. Many of the roads looked like Death Row, since the SS had done their job in finding stray soldiers, executing them for desertion and hanging them from the trees. A washing line of bodies. To see it was horrendous and never leaves you, in fact it comes up in dreams the older you get.

To continue the journey to the Inter shop in Szczecinek we have to creep through the very narrow streets and alleyways. Mappen and I are not amused, since we do not want anything from there. It is wonderful to watch what people will buy, to think that they could get most of the articles of better quality in the West, and very often they do not even need those. Arguments about the prices broke out, but the assistants in the shop were always right.

At long last we are on our way again through the Szczecinek forest into the delightful country side of the lake district. Small ponds, glittering lakes, forests and multi-coloured meadows are passing the window. Round each bend appears a new and wonderful picture. Through the lake district of eastern Pomeranian Switzerland, the Schadower lake appears very soon, deeply embedded in the valley. On the horizon now is the large Prielburger Lake. On its southern tip lies Borne's training ground. Parallel to this road runs the Pomeranian Central Railway, built 1877. This railway encircles the whole of the Pomeranian Swiss. Just as if to order comes now the small two-wagon train round the corner. What a clatter.

Most of the young recruits trained in Borne up to 1944 were later used as cannon fodder to hold off the Russian advance. They were mostly sixteen and seventeen years old by then. Ammunition had already run out, but Hitler in his madness put these young officers to the front to bridge the gap between Küstrin and Frankfurt (on the Oder). They were supposed to fight with clubs and machetes. It would have been better to send these youngsters to the slaughter house. But that was old: now back to the new. At the deep and very ragged shore of the Dratziger Lake lies the peaceful town of Tempelburg (Czaplinek), founded by the Order of the Knights Templar

(Ritterorden). In the flat part of the Zarne in 1754 was the small town of Ratzebuhr, while on the former salt road to Kolobrzeg the town of Bearwalde grew. The most beautiful and romantic part of the area of this lake district was the valley at the top end of the Drage, between Csaplinek and Bad Polzin, now Polczyn Zdroj, lovingly known as "Pomeranian Switzerland", harsh hill sides and sheer drops into the valley with clear waters rushing through. We stopped for a comfort stop and I had a drink from one of those burns, it was exquisite.

The temperature in the bus is now 37 degrees. While the sun plays in the greenery outside, we roast in here. Many heat reflections in various colours and pictures, produced by heat waves, glide over the sandy ground.

Just before Csaplinek is the connection of the two lakes through a large drainpipe from the larger Prielburger Lake to the much smaller Prielburger Lake. After that is a three-way crossing of rail-road-river - most impressive. I for one have never seen anything like it before, a very tidy arrangement and quite easy on the eye and especially perfect fitting into the green landscape.

Near Prielburg at long last we meet lots of tourists and holiday makers. Csaplinek possesses an enchanting old church built from boulders. At first sight it looks very rough, but from nearby one can see the technique and the tremendous skill that went into its construction. The town itself is still an important and idyllic market place for all the products of the region, its market place having mostly old houses. The towerless, new romantic, early Evangelical church, built in the 19th century, hides nearly all of the Catholic church with its adjacent wooden bell-tower. The tower could really do with a coat of gloss, but it survived the first and last war and seemed in use.

Csaplinek itself lies between the Dratziger Lake and the

Tempelburger Lake. In its centre, the 700-year-old protestant church, built in Romanic style, is nearly encircled by little houses. Here we stop for a twenty-minute break. Immediately we are surrounded by children and old folk. Some of the older people stayed on after the war and look nowadays for every bus that comes from the West. Many, however, were resettled here from the other side of Poland. They were re-settled the same way we were, thrown out, therefore understandable That side, the eastern part of Poland, fell to Russia after the Postdam Agreements. A lot of these people have never fully settled here, since they don't see it as their homeland. Again appears one of the new-fashioned buses, a tractor with box. There do seem to be inventors left here with lots of imagination, since these buses have to be seen to be believed. Quite honestly, they fit into the landscape and speed of life here.

The town of Scaplinek had a quieter period of occupation, since the Russian commander stated that no harm was to come to the population if they did as they were told. The number of rapes decreased, if they did not altogether cease.

The valley of the Drage, which encircles the area, is particularly alluring. The gushing wild waters in their dark ravines, sometimes widening into waterfalls, echo through the valley. Between hillocks and sheer slopes of the ridge of the hills lies the white castle "Rosenhöh". Near by stands "Wutzig", the manor where Friedrich von Flatow composed the opera "Martha". This part of Pomerania was fairly difficult for the Red Army to conquer. The narrow and winding roads and forests, hills and ravines were a hindrance. Even our bus has trouble winding its way through,

My mother and Mappen have often rowed on this glass-clear very deep lake. A young lad from the estate, who rowed the boat for them, had so many corns on his toes that his plimsolls had holes cut out to let the corns peep through, it must have been a picture. Today one would have the corns removed, but at that time, under feudal management, he was a peasant and couldn't afford such luxury.

The small hamlet of Alt Draheim nestles between dark lakes. In the old castle, so the guide said, lived a Polish king who had built it, but he couldn't tell us the name. But that fits in with most of the historical things you are told here; there was just no history before the Poles or even before 1945. That Pomerania and Selicia were German for well over 1.000 years is just a figment of the imagination or a twist in history. But to return to the lake. It has a circumference of 70km. The road is very twisting and seems to slope upwards and down. The five lakes have connections through small underground channels, usually not to be seen from above. One can only hear the far away flowing waters.

Bad Polzin (Polczyn Zdroj), an old Moor and Jewish spa is a health resort that has today 7.000 inhabitants and 2.000 holiday visitors. It is an ancient market-town. The park is now over 100 years old. The trees are very much overgrown and long overdue for clipping. Many flowers are already on show and beautifully kept. Many of the houses, some very old and patrician-like, are still there, but all without paint. We found a very appetizing bakery and bought the most fluffy Jam doughnuts and crisp bread rolls, still warm from the oven. The taste was out of this world. It was the smell of newly baked bread that brought the shop to our attention. The Spa Hotel is today a sanatorium. It used to have a large concert-room done out in mirrors, which made it look twice as large. The open-air theatre for plays in summer is quite good and the extensions were just about finished. The park itself was unimpressive, but for walking, very peaceful with its lovely paths and hidden benches.

Eye-witnesses reported that in the region of Pyritz, Arnswalde,

Deutsch Krone, a part of Pomerania south of here, on a farming estate, women and girls were found with stakes rammed through their abdomen. In a butcher's shop a row of naked women with their heads shorn hung on meat hooks. Their stomachs were slit to the abdomen, spilling all intestines, just like pigs. Many women caught syphilis and so did in their own way a service to their womanhood as they passed this then deadly illness on to the Russian armies.

Mappen and the rest of our family used often to be here in the holidays or came to play tennis.The area seems to be the fruit basket here, the trees are in full blossom. Let's hope we have no more frost. On the whole, this is not a very pretty place. The old train from Polczyn to Swidwin was called "der alte Klüter", in English: the old fat, lazy, bulky train. It still does its twice daily service, mainly for schoolchildren. It is very prettily painted.

Mappen's godfather was teacher in Zitzeneff where my grandparents and their children used to be regular visitors. Their visits were always associated with a lot of fun. The master of the mansion had horses and horse-drawn carriages. Ernst, the eldest of the children, found it fun driving through the village pond and so getting everyone thoroughly wet. Ernst enlisted in the First Wold War and was killed at the Somme in France. He went as a volunteer, just nineteen years old. He was the son of my grandfather's first marriage. My first grandmother died of pneumonia when the boy was only three years old. My second grandmother, her sister, took over the household and care of the lad until she married my grandfather. I only remember her as always being ill.

Groß Tydow looks like an overgrown village with its 7.000 inhabitants. Here we have the largest foundling stone in Germany, the "Teufelsstein" (Devil stone). Its circumference is 44m and height 4m. History has it that the face of the devil was seen on the stone. It still looks very awesome with the sun shining on this large, fairly flat, stone monstrosity.

We now reach the delightful cavernous valley, up to 33m deep, of the Persante, between Groß Tydow and Wutzow, very much like our Lake District in England. The old castle in the village of Radue has 99 rooms. With 100 rooms the taxman would have been delighted, since the law decreed that 100 rooms were taxable. Sometime later this law changed to taxing windows. Going by this it looks as if the taxman has always been the winner, even today. Many of the houses and estates built around 1899-1901 have the letters K.v.K., another indication that the von Kamecke family came from here.

Just to provide a change of subject, a very proud heron has just flown over the bus, a most impressive sight, if one thinks that these birds are becoming quite rare. Wonderful is the wingspan and easy sailing through the air of this majestic bird. Just like a small glider.

We are at this moment on our pilgrimage waiting for the believers who are visiting a priests' seminary. The church community of Minden, West Germany, collected money to build the seminary. We sober people are of course making fun of it, since we have not passed a church without stopping to look in it. For church-lovers Poland must be a paradise, since all churches here are really perfect. But the stop here seems to last even longer than usually. The sun is very hot and biting and all our throats are getting parched. The water which we brought is now warm and nearing its end.

And now to the evening meal. Everyone is dirty and very thirsty. It is a lot quieter tonight; everyone seems tired. It has been a very long, dawdling, time-consuming day, sometimes ranging to boring, as looking at too many churches can make one tired of the subject. Sorry people!!

We take a quick shower to finish the day. The shower-bowl, about 70cm by 70cm, with a corner for sitting, has no shower-curtain and only a very few tiles on the floor. Between the unit and the walls is nothing, but empty space. The hand-held shower-head is on a very short lead. A contortionist would have a field day. To top it all the water runs brown after a very short time. Just a quick dab with our kitchen towel, because to get dry with a small piece of material is impossible. Fantastic .... quickly to bed; reading and sleeping, that is the order. Mappen's leg is already packed into its juices and towels, and Mappen in the land of Nod. A full day of excitement and marvellous scenes.

This was now the third day. Just a step back in time!

January 1945.
Posen (Posnan), is burning, East Prussia is burning, West Prussia and Selicia are also in flames. The People of Pomerania are waiting. Into this waiting period storm the hunted and misused masses of refugees from the Eastern provinces. The walkways and alleyways are soon littered with fleeing human convoys. The snow and ice, the bitter cold winds of the winter of 45 are not helping the desperate people who are trying to outrun the masses of the East. The reports these refugees bring are so fantastic that at first they sound unbelievable, but soon prove to be correct.

Killing, ransacking of properties and rape are often reported. Women were nailed alive to barn doors after first having been stripped of their womanhood by numerous soldiers. Women and men were stoned to death. Some French prisoners were clubbed to death. The trekkers reported that the Red Army tanks drove through the columns of refugees, scattering the wagons, carts and people into the sides, or just drove over everything in their way. Right and left of the roads women, children and men, mainly old, were squashed to death, bled to death. The injured cried for help, but tanks have no mercy. Any German soldier found was mercifully shot, while the population was strangled to death in more ways than one. Girls of all ages were raped until they died there and then or suffered another night of agony and unrest to bleed to death the next day under a new onslaught. And all this mostly in the open air, by temperatures below zero. At least they were at peace then.

Many women and children were made to watch the spectacle of mother, sister or daughter being raped again and again, and than being chased into the bitter cold night to meet their death from the frost. All men able to walk were forcibly marched to the East or brutally, inhumanely put to death, until most of the trenches dug were more or less filled with bodies.

All of these deeds were carried out from pure hate and revenge, since the German soldiers had already stamped their mark on the Russian and Polish populations. Their women and children suffered very badly under the German regime. Hate can be a very powerful weapon. According to Stalin's propaganda, the only innocent beings in Germany were unborn children and dogs, and even they were not saved.

The hate propaganda was released by Pravda and Krasnaja Sweda. Whole villages and small towns were completely wiped out. The only thought left after all the population's beliefs were shattered, their trust ruined, their idealism lost in the nightmare was, "Save yourself if you can".

Thousands of babies were left for dead in the snow, since their mothers' milk just froze. The cows' adders also froze and so left no food for the defenceless children. There was no time to bury the little parcels; the ground was by far too hard, the snow and ice too thick. Many women having their babies in the wagons or at the roadside, saw their children die there and then because of the cold. The Red Army actually saw red earth wherever they went, since the snow and ice very often took that colour from the blood.

Stalin's main objective was to reach Berlin in the fastest time, no matter what happened to the civilian population. His propaganda was: "If one day you have not killed a German, you have wasted a day and are likely to die yourself" or "Don't count the kilometres; count the killings and make a pretty carpet".

In a short time all hospitals and reserve hospitals, if they were still in use, were overflowing with frost amputations, pneumonia and diarrhoea. The trains, sledges and wagons, prams and carts were all gradually blocking the transport system generally.

As always hindsight is a wise reaction. If on the 22nd January 1945 the German commander had said that all evacuees, women and children, had to leave the area in provided transport with food and drink at hand, at least 100.000 people would have been spared the horrors and agonies of the following days and months. The German hierarchy, however, did not see it as desperate and even released a memo that anyone would be shot if they tried to leave their homes. In other words, the civilian population was used to delay the Eastern forces. The transport was used to move half a million cigars and 30.000 kg of raw tobacco. 440 train carriages were used to save military equipment which then fell into Russian hands 100km West and was destroyed. Machinery was more important than Hitlers' so called "beloved people".

Many thousands of people were shot by the advancing Red Army just to fulfil their quota of killing Germans; the dead or nearly dead were then overrun by tanks to flatten the ground. It was, all in all, a bloodbath. Eye witnesses reported that people were pushed into a church house which was then set alight. The people being burned to death. The Russians did not burn or destroy churches very often, but the Mongolians seemed to have their fun with it. The ordinary Russian soldier seemed to be in awe of the churches, but no one was allowed to hide in them either, not even the priests.

In front of the Russian advance were the hundred thousands of refugees who blocked all the roads hoping to reach the harbours at the Baltic coast, such as Szczecin. They hoped to make their escape in ships, often pushing their half dead horses to give more. The over laden carts with mostly old or ill people never reached their goal. The wagons or carts were, if lucky, covered with carpets or tent sheets, but the bitter cold of that winter got through with little trouble. If the cold did not do its job, the aeroplanes certainly did the rest. They just repeated what the German forces had done before in other countries and shot wildly into the columns. Fires broke out, people screamed, animals screamed, and so the carnage went on. Another column pushed in front of the armies were prisoners of war from Poland, Britain, France and Bulgaria as so-called cannon fodder.

The whole of the Easter Front could have had strength in its back if only Hitler had listened to some of his real advisers and generals and given then the order for the "Heeresgruppe Nord" to be released from their Kurland positions, that was the area of Lithuania. However, with his tunnel vision and stubborn attitude, he did not believe in defeat, even if it struck one in the face, and therefore left the troops in their northern positions. Hitler never believed that Stalin's force was as strong as it was and propelled by hate, making them a very mighty army in more ways then one. Even when the struggle on the Western Front was already a lost cause, he insisted on every one holding their places and fight to the last man. Had he released the "Rhine Army" at that time, it could have helped to keep the

Russian storm at bay, but they were too far away.

It was therefore not surprising that some of his Gauleiters (District Officials) went beyond the norm in their attempts at law enforcement. One of them was Arthur Geiser. He was made Gauleiter over the Warthegau, and in his view he was now king. He was born in Schroda in 1897, which lies in the county of Posnan. He was brought up, therefore, with the old resentment towards Poles.

The Warthegau came into life after 1939, consisting of Polish-occupied areas and others which had changed nationality,plus East Prussia and the whole of Danzig and West Prussia. It was of a considerable size. Geiser was now working hard to make the Polish people's life Hell. He brought in German farmers and German industrialists, people who had left their Baltic homeland, from Galicia and Bessarabia, which was annexed to Russia.

He was going to integrate the country fully with Germany. The Poles were not to be educated and had to work for their German masters or be shipped elsewhere. After the victory of the Second World War, so it was thought, soldiers and wounded were to receive a piece of land here. He firmly believed Hitler was going to win. Most of the evacuation of the Polish people was carried out by the SS. Geiser was by then "Federal Representative" for the State and Chief of the SS in the Warthegau. He was unshakable in his believe in Hitler and in his name hunted all Poles. He was also a fanatic hunter of wildlife.

He was, however, slightly shaken when he was ordered to install fortifications in 1944. Every able man and all Polish people had to dig and build for a secure future. He never told the population, by now comprising many Germans who had settled there, that one day the evacuation to the West might come. No German or any other human being had to leave the country, or even destroy any property.

He did not evacuate his people at the earliest warning, but he himself left on the 20th January 1945 to go to Berlin for an audience with Hitler. He was, however, never received there. On the 22nd January 1945 he more or less allowed the population to leave. Every train and truck got stuck very soon and many people lost life and limb. Where he was after the war and what his conscience did to him, nobody ever found out, but he got away. Not every Gauleiter was as bad, but many were complete believers and that cost many thousands of lives.

From 1945 onwards it was Stalin who hoped to finish what Hitler had not achieved, the elimination of the Pomeranian nobility.

In 66 cases estate owners and their entire clan were murdered. This part of society also included those imprisoned since the 20th July 1944. Some were shot and left to rot away. Some were driven at gunpoint into their own lakes until they drowned. Others were literally chopped to pieces, the small pieces given to the pigs as fodder. Others still were stoned or tortured until death arrived very slowly. Many died of hunger or illness while others were taken to Russia or Poland for hard labour, ending their lives there. The lucky ones took their own lives, often in the nick of time.

Not very pretty reading, but, unfortunately, very true.

Wednesday May 1985.
The excitement has grown even more today, but we hope that we'll find our return to the old homes a little more friendly and realistic. So far, except for the beautiful country side, Poland has given me the impression of rather sour feelings towards us. How the Poles actually assume that they will always be here is beyond me. They are only the administrators so far, since there

is no peace treaty signed.

After a short dispute as to which Regenwalde (Resko) we want, our journey by taxi starts. On the ancient trading-route back to Ploty, we see a burnt-out Oil installation. The well exploded eighteen months ago and burnt for over two months. Quite a wide area is still blackened. The greenery has suffered a shock to its beauty; all in all everything looks slippery and wasted. It will take a long time for grass to grow here again. Oil drilling in Poland is, to this day, inadequate. The government Department of Energy has tried very hard in different places, because the Polish government needs foreign exchange, which the oil provides. At Polty we leave the main road to turn to Resko. Along the side we come to the first dead trees, the only ones on the whole of the journey, and a forest fire. In Poland itself there are no restrictions on what can be pumped through industrial chimneys. This also applies to the DDR. But, according to the people here, all the pollution comes from the West anyway. About ten kilometres from Resko everything is green again.

Resko is now, as before the war, a small market-town. The church, in which I was christened, is still there, but is now Catholic. The pavements and alleyways are in a deplorable state, with many potholes and no pavement facings. Inside the church the coolness relaxes and revives you. Everything is lovingly cared for and marvellously painted. The font is in full use. It seems as if every stone groans and reaches for life. The inside and outside of all these churches are very often in their original form. The only change that has been made is the language and of course everything is renovated and really looks excellent. The windows are small but in glorious colours. The paving-stones look polished and very well preserved. It is a pleasure, especially if one is a church lover. It is amazing what a Pope can do for the morale of his homeland. It is even more amazing when you think, forty years ago, when they threw us out of here and after that removed quite categorically everything German, they could go and use these churches for their own religion. Pomerania was an Evangelical Protestant country. The Polish population is predominant Catholic and so is this church now.

While the Russians did not actually encourage people to go to church services, the Poles forbade everything to do with the church generally. Services were cancelled, the churches ransacked, the priest put into prison and all that was left were the cries and screams that came from those prisons. Many a priest died a gruesome death. Wherever possible the Russians left the church ornaments. In that respect the Poles behaved quite differently. But as said before, years later they restored everything lovingly for themselves and from what we saw the churches are full.

The market has lost all his old charm and only the housing-blocks replace the old, small, homely, housing area. These large and wide grey-stone blocks make a town very unpleasant and impersonal. It had small houses and picturesque shops before the war, cobblestones all over the market-square, and a tiny pub more or less opposite the church, with large old trees in between; but bombing put an end to these arrangements. My birthplace is not to be found at all any more, in its place is a large housing block. The mill of Gauger and the Hotel Zingler near the Rega, which is the little river flowing through the town, are derelict. With the passing of time this is not a pleasant town any more. It is a pity, as all these small towns took in the farm produce from the surrounding agricultural land before 1945. In this way everyone prospered. The state of the farms nowadays makes such mutual benefit questionable; most people have moved into the towns in any case.

After this depressing inspection, we visit a modern restaurant. Coffee and homemade biscuits are very good. One of the walls is covered with very colourful glass and plastic patches in all shapes and sizes. Our driver and his son tell us it is all crystal, they are blind with false pride and have no feeling for glass or the artificial plastic. They find it absolutely stunning: colourful yes, but primitive and overpowering, not even warm or cosy-looking, just glossy.

The toilets are becoming funnier and funnier. The driver went downstairs first to chase all the men out and then we were allowed to go to the ladies'. He stood guard outside. This was not a toilet for both sexes, they were marked quite clearly for ladies and men. We were also told not to talk to anyone. Cleanliness was, of course, lost again. Why this mysterious behaviour.

When I was a little girl, some years ago, lights and lamps on the streets were not always on, since during the war period too much light was forbidden. So, I can still see my mother coming home the pictures with a large cut on her head. She had walked into a lamppost and cut her forehead quite severely. The scar was forever to be seen. The street lights had just gone off and bombers flew overhead, but at that time they seemed to me just thunder. Hitler's propaganda had really worked; even with bombers coming so far inland the population believed that Germany was invincible.

Our flat was not very big, but very comfortable, the unfortunate thing being that it was one floor up and the pram was a nuisance. Even then and in these circumstances a pushchair soon replaced the pram. I only remember a cosy bedroom with lots of white and pink furniture, curtain and carpet, many dolls, books and other toys, mainly wooden. That was the most usable raw material in just pre-war Germany. They certainly were fun to play with and of course mostly unbreakable. As a teething ring you receive at home a silver ring with an ivory figure on it so it can be chewed on, but as far as I was told, my chewing ring was the wooden elephants tusk. With living in a market town most of the animals were, however, farm animals.

The square used to have very old trees, but has nothing now. It looks bare and against the grey of the houses, boring. Our guide told us sometime that front gardens etc were not good, since they produced nothing, but were good for the eye. Apparently I had a very early introduction to pub-life, since my father used to take me with him for his Sunday walk and beer, that is to say when he was home from the front. I was, unceremoniously sat on top of the bar. This could be the reason why I don't like pubs now.

My only other recollection of the little place is the lovely walks along the River Rega with all the ducks, swans and much more birdlife. The walkway flanked by the water on one side and on the other by bushes and trees and benches for rests or for feeding the birds. Now everything is dirty, run-down and overgrown and no more birds of any size come near or on the river, the smell is horrendous.

Now we proceed further to Swidwin, where the roads are again overgrown with trees which meet in the middle. They do look elegant and give lots of shade. Near Stargard (Starogard) is a large estate, alas, in ruins. A large mansion with plenty of servants' quarters, barns etc. A huge herd of black and white cows is now grazing in the fields, but someone must look after them. So, I must say they don't look lost. The grass is certainly luscious and sparkling greenish.

Further on is Rützenhagen which was a well-known farm estate. Klemzow nearby was also a country estate before the war. Pribslaff, however, a small village, where my grandfather for a long time kept his bees at a friend's home. Bees need the freedom of the country to produce the best honey and as my grandfather lived in the town at that time, conditions were not favourable.

What a lot of wasteland!!! This land was not meant to be built on, but most certainly looks like excellent agricultural ground.

In 1944 and 1945 Swidwin was for many people from the Eastern provinces the end of their journey, since all the trains seemed to come to a standstill here. Everything was blocked with refugees. Because of the tremendous fear of the Russian invasion, the death toll just before the Russian arrival, and shortage of food and shelter, was extreme and unbelievable.

In Three mass graves were many children and women shot by their husbands or fathers, people had hanged themselves in rafters of their homes, or others had taken poison. The Russian troops marched into town on the 2nd March 1945.

Now in 1985 Swidwin has a population of around 25.000. It is 70km from Koszalin away. Two railways keep the town in touch with the outside world.

The buses are flooding into town at the time of the holiday period, since it is not very far from the Pomeranian Switzerland. The River Rega, nowadays very dirty, partly encircles the town and is a magnet for anglers. The Rega springs from the hills of the "Stirnmorane" near Reinfeld and "Mienettchens Ruh". All around the town are forest-covered hillocks, some up to 180m above sea-level. Large and small are inter-connected.

The forests are thick with mushrooms and berries and the air is clean and clear, just perfect for recreation such as walking. Fishing in the Rega is a very popular sport. The extensive forests are a mixture of birch and Scots pine; in between stretch large meadows and waving fields and again clusters of trees in which some of the once beautiful farm estates are hidden. It is a little like fairy-land. Also still quite a few storks.

Since 1954 Swidwin has been a political market-town and this has helped to develop the area. Before that it was under Bialograd's supervision. Shortly after the war the saw mill, dairy- and wine-production were rebuilt and re-developed. Weaving mills and various factories producing goods such as vinegar and mustard, were reopened and the first chemical working-collective was formed. In spite of all the industry, the town is mainly an agricultural centre. Also at home here is a governmental Production Association, which looks after the interests of potato-producers for home use and export. Since 1974 a large animal stud farm has been set up in Swidwin. 4.000 beasts a year are reared for sale or the slaughter house. Swidwin has a grammar school and a technical College and furthermore provides training for agricultural and technical specialists.

In the castle today are the municipal offices, the library, a cafe, a conference-room with 200 seats, an exhibitions-room and a remembrance-room for the Battle of Reinfeld (Bierzwnica). However, this room was organised in honour of all the Russian and Polish soldiers that lost their lives here. For some years running now the poetry competition has been held here. Jan Siewok was the originator; this was truly the first Pole who did anything original here. Reinfeld was a stronghold during the Second World War, where in 1945 very heavy fighting took place. Often the ambulances came to the hospital opposite our home and unloaded the wounded. My mother was always on the look-out to spare us the sight of soldiers arriving, of course she did not always succeed, with serious back wounds and lungs spilling out or with stomach wounds, and all their intestines hanging out. Sometimes arms or legs were missing; heads were split open as if they had been under the cleaver. But our hospital was very small and the pressures from the front were very great. Soon the soldiers were taken to hospitals further in the rear of the retreating German forces.

* * *

The castle is still today an object of interest. It was built between 1286 and 1300 and after that often rebuilt. It stands on the site of the old "Ritterorden" castle. Built on rock the foundations consist of 2,5m thick walls. The fortress like features of the castle are the moat with draw-bridge, the very thick walls and a four-cornered bulwark at the gate. In 1740 the southern part was destroyed by the "Order of the Joanits" and has since then formed the new and comfortable baroque wing. Today's form rose from the reconstruction in 1963 to 1967.

The Gothic church dates from the 14th century. Then the church had only one nave; today it has three. The chapel, the vestry and the organ arrived on the scene in 1475. All are still there. Very much in the building style of the church in Stargard. The main nave with its aisles forms the basilica-like shape.. The beauty of the church is enhanced by the star vault. Two fires played havoc with the building in 1689 and again in 1945. I can remember as we ran past at midday that the burning tower fell to the ground with thundering and hissing noises, not very far from us. It was gruesome and frightening. My mother had tears in her eyes, but not from the smoke alone. The loose burning pieces seemed to follow us on our flight from the inferno. The whole church was a mass of fire. Of the furniture only the granite font remains. Handsome chandeliers decorate the church today

The Steintor (Stonegate) and its fortress-like walls are from the 14th century. A monument in the market-square, large and ostentatious, for the Polish and Russian armies, is certainly out of style here. It takes over the whole place and overshadows all the flowers and even houses. In Memory of the foundation of the Polish army we find a second monument in front of the railway station, namely a fighter plane. The hole made by a Russian tank in 1945 is still in the station wall, not even mended, but some of the cobblestones of the station entrance have been relayed.

Our first duty in Swidwin was supposed to be a visit to the graveyard where my grandmother and the rest of our family are buried. The queue at the florist's was never-ending. While our driver waited for the flowers, we made our way around the original "Kaiserplatz", the Emperor Square.

The old post-office is again doing its duty as such, surrounded by lovely old chestnut trees. The grey house by the post-office was brewer Knuts' domicile. His daughter Erna was Mappen's classmate. Both girls were good runners and competed often and well. Mappen was the best high-jumper and long-jumper in her school. They got some chocolates from the teacher for their efforts. The grey corner house at the corner of Bahnhofstraße and Friedrichstraße, was the prison for a time for a lot of old men, including my grandfather and Herr Kaske, before they were taken to some place to build roads. Most of these men were over seventy years old. The old people were dragged across the country and then lodged with some farmer. My grandfather fell ill and the farmer notified us. His mother had before the war been a customer in Mappen's dressmaking salon. My mother and Mappen dressed as old women with flour in their hair and black clothes and marched off to find him. Charcoal and flour mixed were also used to rub into their faces to give the effect of having a lung disease. The Russians and Poles were extremely frightened of any type of lung illnesses. The two women had hoped to bring him back home, but not at the first attempt. It was forty eight hours before they were back home and we little ones were very frightened. Two of my cousins were with us. We sat in the attic listening to every noise and peeping through the small window to see if they were coming. We were told not to move out of the attic, not to talk loudly or to show our faces anywhere. I really can't remember how we achieved that task. My cousins were three and four years older than us, both girls and gravely in need to see the adults again. The littler one forever in tears and her sister shivering with fright, in case we had visitors. She, being 18 years old, was to take care of us.

The second attempt in Simmering was more fortunate. The Russian officer in charge, however, noticed the charade of the women's clothing, but, because of passes from our local Russian commander, gave the authority. Also that particular officer had an old father near Leningrad. My grandfather was in a shocking state with his clothes torn and his health ruined. It took him a long time to recover at all.

Long marching columns were often herded first to the railway station and then further in animal-trucks, sixty to a hundred people in a wagon. If anyone slipped on the way or even tried to scoop water out of a puddle, he or she was immediately clubbed with a rifle-butt and often shot there and then. Sometimes some more humane soldier would wait until the column was out of sight and with one or two shots finish the job. Wounded or ill people were shot or left to die; there was no point in transporting them anywhere, even if it was only to Siberia. Besides the clothes could be used and they did not have to feed dead people.

The expression "Death at the roadside" had a real significance.

These convoys started shortly into 1945 and thousands of people suffered for a long time afterwards, often until their death, from the clubbing and kicking they had received on their backs and abdomen, even the back of their knees. Often it was impossible to house these masses on their way to Russia, so churches and other accommodations were used. These places had most times no facilities for any personal hygiene and the churches were unrecognisable the next morning. With so many neglected humans it was inevitable that diarrhoea and typhoid broke out. The ones that had not died of malnutrition or other internal illnesses fell foul of these now. Because of neglect in hygiene the flies set in huge hordes and lice arrived in their thousands, both helped along by the warmer weather and longer hours of sunshine. The train-carriages were often not opened for over twenty four hours. Many people simply went mad, others died where they stood or were left where they lay. This made the stench even more unbearable. Disease was spreading even faster.

In these horrendous conditions, with most women and girls ill of one disease or the other, they were still free to be hunted and used by the now Polish partisans that herded on the trains and most times ransacked the same. The only ones at peace were the dead ones and most people envied them. They also came to realise what their own soldiers must have done to the Russian and Polish populations.

One of the earlier atrocities of 1939 was the "bloody Sunday of Bromberg", where Polish civilians were clubbed to death in the streets by uniformed German hoodlums, hanged from lampposts or chased out of the town, that now belonged to the "Reich".

The monument at the Kaiserplatz has now a cross where previously "Kaiser Wilhelm" stood. The kiosk on the corner is now a large, filthy supermarket. The "Steintor" often photographed from all sides, still stands on its foundations and seems proud of it.

Tasteful flowerbeds and lovely parks line all the way to the Kolbergerstraße. On the corner of Steinstraße, on the ground floor, was the "Pommersche Bank" (Pomeranian Bank), where Mappen learnt the banking business. The next landing was occupied by a solicitor called Schubring. On the top floor was Director Lotz. In the next house was Albrecht's lingerie shop, even long before the war a very fashionable place. Then came

Klatt's house, which always had beautiful porcelain. The next house was owned by two Jews named Lewis. They always got honey from my grandfather; they were also among the first Jews to disappear from the town. Last but not least Puchstein's large book shop. Part of the new supermarket stands on the site of the old house, where the ravishing and very available miller's wife lived. Even at that time humour existed. Next was Ponart, who had a mill in Beustrin.

The school where my grandfather taught was nearly the same as I remember it, just even greyer. He was here for many years. All his children attended it. His study was just over the main door and has today closed shutters. I wondered how the kitchen would look and silently thanked the old staff for the food we were once provided with.

A lot of new buildings and new installations were built in Bergstraße, including the length of Glasenabstraße to the promenade where Pieper's sawmill was.

Well, at long last the flowers arrive and we are off to the graveyard. Everything in the German cemetery is devastated. The grass has taken over; even the grave border-stones are missing. It seems that everything was carted off. It is a scandal for a Catholic country not to honour the dead. A graveyard is supposed to be sacred and of course history, but not here in Poland.

Just left of the chapel Mappen measured in steps where the graves should have been. She then dug a small hole with her hands to plant the flowers. It was heartbreaking to see how an old lady (she is now eighty years old) tried to find her own mother's grave and of course those of the other relatives. We stood for a little while, said a silent prayer and hoped that somewhere the thoughts were received. After all this it may seem strange to read that Mappen sends parcels to a Polish family so they don't starve and are properly dressed. Somehow the world is twisted, because I shall not be able to understand it. I hated these people at that moment. They threw us out of our homeland at one time and, to make it worse, ruined the country after that. The inheritance that these people took over has been completely wasted by them; nobody wants to work here, but most of them are fat and round. There is enough energy to produce super large families, which however they cannot feed. On the other hand, however, these people did not start the war. It has come to light, that if Hitler had not taken Poland, the Poles would have started an uprising anyway. Elaborate preparations to overthrow the occupiers had been taken by the Polish underground and were then in place. Patience would have been the better part of valour. The war would most likely have come, but Germany would not have been the main instigator and thus the recipient of all the blame. Unfortunately the older generation did not think so far. As said, hindsight is always good.

Some of the Russian prisoners-of-war from the Crimea were left in Swidwin and tried to greet the Red Army as friends. They put garlands around their houses and went out of their way to greet them in the streets with bread and salt. The soldiers however laughed at them from their tanks. Their reaction was to cock their guns and just mow down the old farmers and their women as they tried to give them the plates. These farmers had lived a long time in a country where they were second best and were pleased to see their own folk again. We onlookers also were absolutely shocked. The snow turned to the colour of blood, bright red.

It is getting late, since the flower shop has wasted so much of our time. We carry on through the Bahnhofstraße to the corner where butcher Möller had his shop and slaughterhouse.

On the 2nd March 1945 we found ourselves in the late

afternoon on these premises. It was the day the Mongolians marched in. All afternoon we could hear the rattle of machine-guns and the thunder of tanks as they rolled down the streets. The blasting noise and the cold fingers of fear were tremendous. Just three women, trying to be brave and composed outwardly, but shaking with fright and uncertainty, trying to huddle together with a number of small children. The now empty and clean stalls, where only days ago cows had stood awaiting slaughter, were useful to hold this flock of lost sheep and help us to warm each other. It is amazing how cold it gets when one is frightened. How we all got there I have no idea.

We children were not allowed to cry in case it would be heard from the outside. The darkness and the cold soon sank into our clothing and the children started to whimper, but the noise seemed to move; with short breaks it lasted all night. It seemed as if all the evil forces were let loose and had descended on this piece of earth. Chalk dust and soot and black flakes together with water drops fell from the ceiling. The building was swaying and cracks appeared in a far wall, but it seemed to hold. The human being is very small in the face of these unleashed forces. Bombs fell and shells dropped all around, but the slaughter-house was built like an old fortress with immensely thick walls. The whole Earth seemed to move. As we came out in the morning light we saw the destruction of the houses, the corner of the slaughter house was missing. A grey haze hung over the streets and over the whole town. Instead of snowflakes, black flakes of burning wood were floating around.

In the middle of the main street was the body of a Russian general. He cost many people their lives, since he was apparently shot in the back, and as general belief had it, with a small handgun. Six weeks the raping and plundering lasted. The doors had to be opened day and night for Russians, mostly drunk and very dirty. We were not allowed out of the house at this time. Nobody knew we were in my grandfather's house and everyone had to speak in whispered tones. We children were hidden behind the coal in the cellar. It was a dark time. At night we were often rolled into blankets and laid along the bottom of the beds as if it was just another cover.

A commander soon ended the horror. He put a sub-commander in charge of every street and a sort of eerie silence hung over the town. But not for long. Then the Polish armies arrived. Mongols had been bad enough, but the Polish hordes knew no restraint.

It was getting more difficult to find hiding-places, since the Poles even climbed into burnt-out cellars, as long as there was a chance they could find women and girls, often no older than seven or eight years. Old women were not safe either, up to seventy five years old, and after their ordeal they were drowned in the River Rega, shot, or manhandled until death came as a relief. There was no way of fleeing, since the ones who tried had a terrible life afterwards, if they got caught. Many women saved their lives by literally offering themselves to the Russian or Poles - better one man than regular hordes of drunks. It even transpired that a Russian commander called a halt to the marauding, but that did not last very long either and the old carnage was once more in full swing. So-called horror films of today are nothing compared to what we saw and heard, and because of these two senses, imagined. A child's mind is very efficient in its filing system.

But I digress from the horrors of that day. From the slaughter-house we ran past the burning church towards the River Rega, via the market place and some small streets. The noise and roar of the flames was quite tremendous. The crackle of wood and falling masonry was very frightening and real. All these sounds intermingled with the shouting of foreign voices make everyone gather their reserves of strength and run, often into the guns of the enemy. To run for one's life is invigorating, frightening, a relief in doing something, but mainly the urge to get away from the town that is folding together like matchbox buildings. The burning and hissing of flames is an unforgettable experience. It seems to follow everywhere, since everywhere everything is in flames.

The station is again rebuilt and looks fairly presentable, except for the grenade hole that was shot into it in 1945. The aeroplane in front does not really belong there. It is a memorial for the dead pilots. The battle for Swidwin was fierce.

We go on to the old monastery now, where the "Plumpe" (outside water pump) still stands. The house from the outside is a mess. My mother was born here. Mappen and her brother Hans have many happy memories from their childhood here. The shed, or barn, was burnt out two weeks ago. A young couple occupy the premises now, with their parents living next door. The living quarters are renovated, papered and painted. On the floors are reasonable carpets. In the living room stands a cabinet full of crystal and very old German pre-war goods. These until recently used to receive parcels from friends of Mappen. The Polish women were, however, so unreasonable while visiting the West German couple in Bad Segeberg that the parcels came to an abrupt end. Mother and daughter arrived one day at their West German house and said that they had come for a holiday. The two women then went within one week first to the dentist, then the optician and after that to every specialist they could find. The bills were all sent to Mappen's friends after the women had left. The pair went shopping every day to buy tyres for their old Mercedes in Poland, plus every other article they could think of. Mappen's friends found out just by chance, when one bill arrived which neither of the women had been able to hide. Forty seven bills eventually turned up to a total of DM 12.482,--. By then, of course, the women had been put on the boat at Travemünde back to

Poland. The friends said, "Never again!"

All the park by the monastery has gone. The swimming-bath behind the house is still there, but the river is extremely dirty. A rowing-boat lies lost and lonely, with rotten boards in the water. The garden is in very good order. On the whole these people are very likeable. We are given tea and invited to stay. Afterwards we found out that they wanted more parcels, but this time from us. Wherever they could get addresses from the West they turned up on the doorstep one day and ran up huge bills in the occupier's name. When they had bought everything anyone could think of, they left for their homeland with all the goods. Twice it happened that they had to hire a van to take them to Travemünde for their boat. My aunt, however, did not take up the request. She already sent parcels to Polish people in the town.

Behind the monastery lies the estate of Größlin from where the Russians came that fatal day in 1945. We were by then lying along the river behind a dyke, our faces black from soot, our hearts thumping from the run through town. Every time one of us moved our heads, they fired at us, or so it seemed. The continuous fire was horrendous. The exploding grenades struck deep and splattered the snow and mud everywhere. The noise was overpowering. It was all a nightmare, but unfortunately it was only the beginning. In front of us, over the river, were a large field and a hay barn. It was a hiding-place for a number of people, young and old. We saw the Russians on their horses galloping into the barn, shooting and stabbing everyone they could find, regardless of whether they were women, children or even elderly people. They seemed to take great pleasure in riding their small horses at full gallop into the unarmed crowd. It didn't matter who got underfoot. While we were lying behind the wall of mud, women and girls were dragged out and sexually assaulted before they were thrown back into the barn or into the River Rega, to be killed or maimed by horses' hooves or bayonets. The cries were appalling. An old man came out of the barn and pleaded with the officer. He was promptly shot. A young woman, who screamed and kicked whilst being raped, was tied by her feet behind a horse and dragged behind it at full speed and to laughter of the soldiers, until she fell unconscious. She was a terrible sight when they threw her into the river.

A woman came out of the shelter with her baby in her arms. She shouted something in her mother tongue (the Russian language of the Crimea) and showed them the baby. The soldiers tore off her clothes and underwear until she stood naked in the freezing cold, still holding her baby tight in her arms. "Davai!" was the cry from the soldiers, and they immediately picked up the woman and threw her back into the hay. The baby was thrown into the snow where it died. The woman screamed and fought with the soldiers, but to no avail. After a long while the inhuman howling stopped. Her naked body was covered with blood, her breast were partly torn off, her face was flattened. They had stamped their boots on it and into it. Her head was literally kicked in, a picture one never forgets. About a dozen Red Army soldiers must have taken that woman, one after the other. There was just nothing left of her to classify her as a human being. I can partly understand the Russian attitude; they had suffered similar cruelties to their people, but were we, as children, to know that?

Too many Russian citizens had starved, were evacuated or killed in the years 1942 to 1945 for the forces not to be filled with hate and disgust towards the Germans. The Russian and Polish soldiers often had pictures of their murdered loved ones with them and showed them to their victims while ill-treating them.

Many French prisoners-of-war were still in these areas and helped the civilian population wherever possible. Many lost their lives for it, since the Eastern forces did not separate enemy from friend.

Many Russians, mainly from the Ukraine, evacuated from their homeland 1941 to 9142 into German as a labour force, were not now safe from their own people. Often these poor creatures stood between their overlords and the incoming forces. Many times, however, the Ukrainians helped the German civilians. They had a good life under the Germans and tried in their own way to repay. This was when life took another twist in human relationships. We had a young man from the Ukraine with us for a long time. I still have his medallion, a girl's face on a mother-of pearl background. I have it on a chain - why, I don't know - but it gives me a sense of peace. Whatever happened to him, nobody knows.

All in all, it was a time one never forgets. What my mother, brother, my grandfather and I saw that day and even lived through is now, even after thirty-nine years, still unbelievable. When I see this and now and think that my brother and I were born here, there does not seem to be any connection at all. Now these people wreak havoc with this land. No small wonder that my family had a fine and safe childhood here, if one ignores all the rubbish the Poles have created.

After a desperate attempt at crawling on hands and knees, we soon had to abandon this and try to run. A small path brought us in 1945 to a very small bridge. I think it was a tree trunk, but I can't be sure, since I don't remember that bit too clearly. All I remember is being chased by the enemy on horseback. The jungle along the waters' edge saved our lives. But as usual when you are running it never seems fast enough. With our small bundles and the closeness of the undergrowth it was not a race I should like to run again. Thank God the undergrowth was too marshy for the little horses to follow. We were absolutely wet through and through and that with the tremendous cold, but so far we were alive.

During all the running and hiding in the bushes you had to hold your back bent or be hit by gunfire from behind. The tanks were still rolling into Swidwin at a vast rate and they did not bother if anything was in their way. To think now we must have run literally for our lives! All I can remember is falling into bushes a lot, very thick bushes, falling and tumbling again into the undergrowth until darkness was setting in. The tanks were still firing over our heads, but the distance had increased and we were by now under the high arch of the shells and therefore safer to move out. Dirty, hungry, thirty, tired and with shaking legs and sodden wet clothes, it is a wonder we never caught pneumonia, but nervous exhaustion must have kept illness at bay. And always: "Sh! Sh!" I don't know if it was cold, but the winter of 1944 was bitter.

With hiding in alleyways and door recesses, creeping from street to street, around every tree that was not burning, listening for every voice, footstep or any other noise, we made in deep darkness for the school, sometimes on hands and knees and always very slowly, After that just around the corner to friends of my grandfather's, where we found shelter for the night. Everything smelt of soot and felt hot. Everything was out of context. Many people were in that house that night. No light could be lit, since the Russians would have known that people were in the house. The area had been searched and cleared of people by the forces earlier in the day, since the Russian forces set up their camp around the market square and the immediate side streets. This house had been bombed and we all stayed in the still warm cellar. Early the next morning my grandfather and I ventured out to find food. The school was not far away. One of the wings was used as a Technical High School and therefore had kitchen facilities. Moreover it had not been plundered or burnt or even occupied and the kitchen was loaded with assorted foods. A gross oversight by the Russians, but then they went more for the breweries. We carried some of it back and bit by bit we were able to feed all the hungry faces in the cellar, with some food. Two other old people joined in the hunt. Always one had to be on the lookout to avoid any patrolling soldiers, but the final result was that everyone got something in their stomach. From there we set out much later in the day, with some of the other occupants, in the direction of my grandfather's house. The day was grey and overcast and by then very cold. It was already early evening. After the hectic night and the vast amount of drink, the Russians had to sleep all day and the roads were fairly quiet. My grandfather had the sleeping Peter in his arms. It was nevertheless a grim journey.

My grandfather was at that time seventy years old, a very sprite seventy, and events took their time. He was worn out from the day before and, of course the mornings hunt. We had again to be extremely careful and quiet, seek all the little alleyways, climb through burnt out places and feel every step one made in case of potholes. It seemed to take ages, but that could have been the tiredness from the day before, because the distance to his house was not far.

In front of the house, however, was a very drunken Russian soldier, holding a loaded gun, waving it about, but not able to aim at one thing properly. His little eyes, set in red-rimmed sockets were rolling in all directions. In his filthy clothes he looked a menace and fright overtook all of us. We hid behind some bushes for while, but he must have taken our movements in, since he made his way on very unsteady legs in our direction. He had the well-worn trousers and dirty Cossack top which all troops wore. He smelled horrendously. He was not very tall, but his gun at such close quarters made him appear huge to me. My mother had a small hand gun, but froze; she could not pull the trigger, which my grandfather had already cocked before we left the other people. She had enough ammunition for all four of us. My grandfather just shouted

"Shoot, girl!" I pulled my mother's finger and the person in front of us was crumpling down. God knows how, since it was impossible to take aim at that moving figure. There was just a large amount of blood, but I don't remember where it all came from. It is still a blur. I was seven years old and that was my first, and last, victim. Luckily that escapade did not scar me, but that is where I think a sense of survival started for me. Automatically you are drawn into something that does not really concern you. You are too young and small to understand the really cruel life of that time, your main concern should be playing. Maybe that was just as well!

During the hours of darkness my grandfather buried the man under the frozen compost heap in the garden, the other ground was too hard. We were waiting all night for a patrol to knock on the door. We were very lucky and relieved that no one else saw what happened. The road was completely empty, but just 300 metres away the tanks were grouped and waiting for a new onslaught. My mother was crying and very white and shaking. She was a warm hearted and loving person, and could not reconcile herself with the fact that she had not been able to pull the trigger when needed. It also was against her nature that a dead soldier was lying under our compost. Her main dread was, what would happen, when the Russians found one of their own missing. Out of that skirmish, my real remembrance is the longing for the beautiful peace of lying in a warm bed and being allowed to go to sleep.

When we finally got into grandfather's house it was a terrible mess, the smell was horrendous. Everywhere we looked were piles of human excrement. The bath was full of filthy clothes; even the toilet was stuffed with clothes. All the rooms were ransacked, that is to say, everything was thrown all over the floor – why, we never found out, which was just as well, because if there had been a second visit the soldiers would have taken the rest as well, and most likely have molested my mother or my aunt, or come to that possibly even me. A pigsty would have been a cleaner place. Our beds were in the attic and hidden from searching eyes. There also used to be my aunt's dress making rooms, but they were reached by a different entrance and the stairs were blown away, but they could be reached from inside if you knew how.

This must have been the worst day so far in my short life, and because of that, the warm bed and sleep were immediate and heaven. Every child likes to pretend things are not as bad or as different as they really are, and most likely at that time pretence took over my young mind.

Back to the journey:
Our next stop is Buchholz Lake, wonderfully enclosed in forest, an idyllic lake now with holiday chalets, but only for small people; the chalets look minute. The open-air theatre is out this world, colourful, and even romantic looking. Everything awaited the unsuspecting holiday makers. A lovely white beach, like sugar, surrounds the lake, restaurant and cinema are on the same premises. Only at this time, May, the facilities are closed. It is the ideal spot and easily reached by foot from Swidwin. On our way back we visit, first my grandfather's house, as expected, in need of repair and paint. The mature gardens now partitioned and bordered with high wooden fences. Fair enough - it was a very large garden, but now there are three made of it and none of the old fruit trees are left, nor bees nor beds of black tulips along the garden wall. The back-yard is a real shambles. The outhouse is near collapse; my swing would not be safe here now. It used to hang on the large door-beam high above the ground, the rings are still there. Three parties share the house now. Grandfather's flat now houses a lady gynaecologist, who has at least painted the balcony. A small corner of the roof was damaged during the war by tank ammunition and is still damaged today. Three corner tiles were shot off and left a hole on the edge of the roof.

To our amazement it was stuffed up with a blanket. The fall pipe for the guttering was breaking off in 1945, and has to this day not been repaired. It looks very rusty and messy.

Can't people see that their property needs running repairs? Surely it is not assumed that early things keep themselves in good order. Where the rainwater spreads out from the fall-pipe the body of the Russian soldier lay many years ago. The compost heap is gone. Whoever did the digging must have had a terrible shock when they found the human bones. But, on the other hand, there were so many graves that one more would not have made any difference, or so I told myself. After all, it had been self-defence. Not only did they find bones, but also all our silver. It was wrapped up in cotton wool, towels and canvas to keep it safe for us until after the occupation. Alas, that was not to be.

Diagonally across the road was the Kindergarten, where later the Poles lived in their Officer's quarters. It is now an official building bearing the Polish Eagle. During the war the same building was for a time used as a hospital. I was, apparently, a constant visitor to the kindergarten before the occupation, at the age of three to five years old. If Gitty was not to be found, that was the first place to look. I cannot think why I was not enrolled as an inmate? If someone is so determined to play with other children, it would have been, for me anyway, the solution. My grandfather played Father Christmas there in the winter of 1943, but I am afraid that has slipped my memory. I do remember Christmas 1944, We got beautiful skis, my brother and I, also a whole wooden zoo of carved animals, and, as a special treat, a rag doll. That was the last time we had a Christmas tree for quite a number of years. The skis did not get used a lot, since the occupation started soon afterwards. I do know, that we tried them out on the little hill next to the house. There was not a lot of traffic at that time and my mother watched. The hill was used by us for sledging in any case and therefore not new to us. Taking the sledge to the top and running it down made one go right across the main street into the old hospital garden. If one was lucky, straight through a hole in the hedge and further into the field. But cars were no hazard in 1943-44. Even my mother was quite pleased with our activities and presumably out of her hair for a while. I do remember that there were some other children, but I think they were slightly older. But snow has no barriers when it comes to age. That slope was just perfect for sledging.

That Christmas my grandfather, my brother and I went into the forest to get what was to be our last Christmas tree. It was a beauty, tall and even shaped. When the candles were placed on it, it was fantastic. Even now, we have real candles on our Christmas trees. It makes the festive season more gorgeous, seasonal and to me homely. My Scottish husband is very much in favour of the old traditions. The one feature missing most years is the snow, of which we had plenty in Pomerania.

As I now stood in front of where our house used to be, seven houses away from my grandfather's, I could hear again the cluster bomb that landed in our back garden. It made a fantastic hole in the ground. Two parts of the cluster did not explode. The third part of the monstrous metal construction pointed towards the house. Then a dead silence set in, lasting for a few minutes; even the rattle of the flak seemed to have stopped for a little while before the fire-engines with their sirens howling echoed along the street. The rest of the bomb never did explode. Whatever happened to it later, I can't say. Everything happened so fast that we did not even get into the bunker. This particular bomb seemed to have been an isolated case that day. We did stare at it for a few days and then.... I don't know.

The other memory I have of that house is that after the Russians found pictures of Adolf Hitler next door in the ground-floor flat, they set fire to the house. For us, it was quite a shock. When we came next day to see what was left of our house, we found our cooker, all white, standing on top of all the rubble. Just like a large chimney. Needless to say, we left it there. We were staying at my grandfather's house, the rattle of gunfire, fire and the rumble of falling masonry had alerted us of the tragedy. It was a six family house and left a huge amount of black rubble. It moaned and groaned for quite a few days. To my mother it was a huge shock, since having already lost my father, she had lost now her home as well. The people in the ground floor flat actually burned to death in their rooms. Some of the other occupants had already left. Some of them, that was one family, on the last train out of Swidwin a few months prior. I think from then on my mother realised that things were going downhill. She seemed to get depressed and often very cross with us, or so it seemed. At that time we could not understand it, but now, yes it really makes sense.

The bunker itself is still quite clear in my memory. Every air attack seemed to bring out the shelter supervisors with their cries of "It is law to get into the bunkers". Across the road from flat was the hospital and after that just large fields. Under the hospital, towards the back, the bunker was constructed. A few steps underground and endless corridors with benches along the sides were the complete lay-out. The smell of the smoke from the bombs, the sweat, the noise of the crying children, the whispers of the adults so the children would not hear the grown-ups' fears, even the roar of the aeroplanes and the howling of the sirens came down here, all through the air shafts of the hospital. These were more feelings of hopelessness than actual memories in detail. As my mother told me later, some people prayed, some played cards and others spoke of everything but the war, which to some of them had not even arrived. It was a time to block out the present. Even a sharp argument was a relief of tension and frustration, while overhead the flak thundered and bombs exploded. Fire sirens tended to drown out all the other noises, but to no avail. Many people seemed to run in and out all the time during the siren alarms. On leaving the shelter, everyone seemed to have aged, was extremely dirty and somehow deflated. Now they had to find out what was still standing of their houses, since down here they had only heard the thunder of bombs, very often very near. The only ones to be relieved to get out of those confined spaces in the bunker seemed to be the children, of course, they did not know of any danger all those noises could cause.

To this day the feeling of fear follows me in enclosed spaces. At that time you felt the dark and the cold, and someone always saying, "It's alright darling," didn't reassure a six-year-old little girl for too long. My mother's eyes gave a lot away. My father was at that time already dead at the Russian front, and our hope that he would be back soon was in vain; so all this was a passing phase.

One day, however, that passing phase got louder. It made a tremendous rumble and the ground seemed to rock. The bombers came in large groups and discharged their loads over our town. The little place was already overrun with refugees from the hinterland. The market-place was badly hit. My aunt's house and shop, a material shop with dress making facilities, was in ruins. Many more houses went up in flames. Food was getting shorter and more and more people left the area. Even our evacuees from Herne in the Ruhr district left for home, where it was now safer than here. We had a lady teacher as an evacuee, and when she returned to her homeland she wanted my mother and us children to go with her. She had the foresight to realise that the Eastern front would not hold out much longer. She boarded one of the last trains to leave Swidwin and still reach the Ruhr, maybe. She looked very lost and forlorn in her dark clothes and very strict hair style. She was an elderly lady and we never saw her again. Shortly after her train had taken the long journey, all transport stopped here, even the fields and forests were blocked with fleeing people. People seemed to appear from everywhere and sleep or stand on any spare place. Food and water as well as medical supplies were running short already, since the refugees had flooded back and forth for some time now.

After the day of disaster, we were to witness the most horrendous spectacle. A quite horrific scene developed as a group of bombers dropped their fire bombs over Szczecin, about 75km away to the northwest. My brother Peter, my mother and I stood at the living-room window in our flat, where we children admired the "falling Christmas trees". The whole sky was lit up and it really looked like trees falling, a fireworks display nobody could imagine in colour and formation. These bombs were filled with phosphorous. The elements lit up the whole horizon and were seen many miles away. Even at that time no one thought the war was so near to our doorstep. Shortly afterwards, on a sunny but cold day, the horrors of war really arrived. The most essential things were packed and everyone had a small parcel for emergencies. Back into town we go past the saw-mill, where the Russians forced my grandfather to give up his watch at gunpoint.

"Uri! Uri!" was their continual cry. They very nearly shot him, when they saw that the watch was in his shoe and part of the strap was visible over the rim. Only the excitement of getting the watch saved his life. They danced with pleasure. I can still see the whole of the promenade blocked with tanks, lorries and jeeps filled with Russian soldiers. It seemed that there were millions of them with their, to us children especially, horrible, harsh language.

The soldiers were Mongolians, even to us little ones they looked more square and short than the rest of the adults. Their dirty and worn-out uniforms did not make them more commendable either, but these men and women had come many thousands of miles here through all sorts of terrain and weather. But what would a child do with reasons like that? The adults were frightened and in a way disgusted with the enemies appearances. They seemed threatening, and that was also mirrored in everyone's face.

One of the first nights of the occupation, there was knock on the front door, since the bell for the house had been dismantled by the very first wave of soldiers. My grandfather went to open and outside stood three Russian officers. Our hearts sank to our feet, but the men were silent and official looking. They came in with their muddy and heavy gum-boots and made themselves at home. They inspected the large flat and its surroundings very thoroughly. After a while we found out that one of them wanted to have a room. He was going to stay with us for the rest of his tour. Shock again. We had heard what had happened to other families with Russian tenants. However, it turned out that he was one of the few high-ranking officers with charm and honour. He was an opera singer and came from Odessa. He was married, with two little boys, whom he missed very much. Our Peter was soon his favourite. My mother's first reaction was horror on more than one account. The man was a stranger; too many children just disappeared never to be seen again. So what next?

He, however, just sat there combing the boy's hair and feeding him Russian chocolate, singing a Russian lullaby. My mother was stunned. He had the most filthy comb, a most kind face but an extremely sad expression. He brought us food, lard, marmalade as well as jam, chickens and bread. He made sure that no one entered the premises. He really had a most kind nature and loving charm, together with a very soft melodious voice. He did not speak any German and the conversations were conducted through drawing everything. When he had another parcel of food under his arm we had all to sit around the table and watch him unpack his goods. It was like meeting

Father Christmas. His delight of producing these goods was mirrored in his face and he used to accompany his unpacking with lovely songs, while my mother had to play on the piano.

We got passes, that is the adults did, children did not exist, and were not allowed on to the roads. To compare our lives with some of the other families', we were super lucky while he was there. The looting, raping, murdering that was going on was indescribable. Most days and nights one could hear the screams of the women and whimper of children from other houses along the street. Often in the morning someone else was missing. We children were not allowed to go onto the street at all, even with him. The back garden was our only domain and then only quietly.

The officer stayed with us for about five months. He often joked about the first night in his rudimentary German or pictures, because I was at that time rolled in a blanket, with my legs under me, so that I looked more like a very small child than a six-year old. He found it very funny, but I did not. It is very uncomfortable being stuffed into a cot and it is very painful having your legs tied behind you, like Long John Silver. But anything was a good measure to protect a young girl, a child, a human being. My brother was often hidden at the bottom of the bed. Nothing and no one was safe from the Russians and their militia women. If one can say luck held out, it certainly did for us during all those long months. Food was not plentiful, but we had some every day. We also had peace at night and day. Many children were abducted to Poland and Russia. Many young girls, of eight years onwards, were raped and then left to die. When there was a purge on, they came and searched the houses and stabbed with their sabres along the edge of the beds, into wardrobes, really every corner where anyone could have hidden, and all this under the officers' supervision. Even that was out of the ordinary, since no one else had this protection. He was our protector and to this day we are grateful. The carnage that went on in other houses was horrifying. He played our guardian angel. My grandfather had to accompany him very often, since he seemed to know his way of thinking and understood the drawings the Russian produced. In this way we got to know of goings on in the district. But it helped also some other families, since my grandfather was known in Swidwin, and could therefore help some in their predicament.

Mappen had to sew for the Russian officers' wives or their camp followers. For the first time in their lives these women had new hand made clothes. The only thing my aunt had to be careful of, was not to make one dress better or prettier, because the women fought like alley cats otherwise. Hair flew everywhere and tooth marks were not uncommon. Their militia women were by far the worst and of course the dirtiest in all respects, that is to say just behind the Polish militia. Lice and other body bugs, as well as genital deceases were common order.

The Russian headquarters were in the Reichsbank. It was cleaned by a large force of German women. At the beginning of the occupation many of these women were shipped to any eastern sector, often leaving children and elderly relatives in the morning, never to return in the evening or night. Later on the same women turned to being personal friends of some of the officers and men and so saved their lives and those of their families. The forces attached to headquarters kept their women away from the Army. It was not a happy life that these women had, but it was a way of survival.

Our officer would sing the most melodious Russian lullabies and ballads. All the Russian heavy sentiment seemed to lie in his voice. He also gave musical renditions to the family and chosen officers, with my mother accompanying on the piano. My mother had studied music for four years before her marriage. She was a qualified music teacher for seven instruments. She also gave her own concerts.

Our officer was very fond of my grandfather, but there he was not alone, for we all loved him. He was very strict, but very fair. Because of that he insisted that the officer should eat with us. This he did, but only if he had previously brought the food. So, even that turned on itself. That man shared every scrap of food with us. He did not provide a vast amount of food, but most days brought something with him, often just for us children. We were very sad to see him go. But with him also went a very large number of militia women and the town was quieter for a very short spell. Then the new hordes arrived on our streets, namely the Poles. They had arrived in town about six weeks before, but had ransacked and molested other areas first. They did their pillaging and terrifying mostly during the night, and it seemed very thoroughly. Often including burning the buildings down if they did not found any or enough loot.

After the peaceful occupation with our Russian officer, we got a Polish officer. He was a very insignificant person of small stature. He had to have right away two large rooms. The Russian officer was a tall man and needed only our smallest room, this small man however, needed the two largest. He ate everything he could find. The only good thing he did was to brew his own "Schnaps", that is a clear spirit made from corn or potatoes. When he was out we used to fill a spare bottle with some of the liquid and fill his large brew up with water. That stuff was 90% alcohol, clear as water and to us the best medicine. He then caught typhoid and insisted that my mother nursed him. When, however, it got too bad my grandfather went to the Polish headquarters and put forward his case. They were appalled, since that illness had to be reported. We had to put a second sign on the door "Typhoid". He was transferred to the hospital. While all this went on we still had the sign outside stating that we had Russian lodgers. Not all the Russians had left, so that little piece of paper was not outdated in that respect. Nobody had thought to take it down and we did not remind anybody. It brought normality to the household for a while, in spite of our not being able to leave the premises. It was so good to have the run of the house. We also made sure that we ate the last chicken before the Polish officer came out of hospital. *It was difficult to hide the ch*ickens when he was there, but it is amazing what can be done. As I said before, we children slept in the attic and so did our chickens. Grandfather build them a small run and we fed and watered them there.

At the end of March 1946, this being towards the end of the second wave of evacuations, our Polish officer had us thrown out of Pomerania. There was no more food for him and this having been reported to the authorities, we were no good to him any more. How long he stayed in the house we don't know.

Years later, my mother and I saw our Pole again in Lübeck (West Germany). He was walking along the promenade of the River Trave. When he saw us he ran. How extraordinary! He limped. Even in Swidwin he walked with this limp. We were sure it was he. Why should he have to run otherwise? Besides, no-one had so crooked a face. He got away; my mother was disappointed. She had regained some her strength and I know she would have attacked him one way or another. What was he doing in the West? Espionage? My aunt tried to convince us that she saw him in Lübeck, but she didn't even live there. My reason for not believing that one, was that she and my grandfather were moved to Varel in Friesland and then on to Jever shortly after we all arrived in Lübeck. They never came to live in the camp, that is to say my grandfather visited us for a short spell later.

February, March and April 1945:
About 50% of the Pomeranian population fell into the hands of the Red Army on their entry into the province. It has been

proved that of all the provinces east of the Oder and Neiße the plan for destruction through fire and other devastation did this province the most damage. It is also right to say immediately after their entry into Pomerania the devastation by the Red Army was more gruesome than the damage done by bombing and fighting.

Immediately after the entrance of the Red Army the pillage and ransacking were at their highest level. It was all done very efficiently. Just before the winter attack of 1944-1945 it was released from the Soviet High Command that it was allowed to send as many parcels as possible to Russia.

At the conference in Yalta Stalin tried to get approval for the shipment of German folk to Russia to work in their mines and their forests. The evacuation, however, started before this approval was ever agreed. March 1945 saw the high point of the evacuations. On the whole, all men to the age of 60 were deported. If, however, the number for the day was not large enough in some towns or villages, women had to go as well. The deportations were in the hands of the Soviet military forces.

The deportation camps were terrible places, run by individual fighting forces. No food was offered during long marches in the bitter cold winter often for days on end. The people were just herded as cattle. Thousands of men and women died on these marches. In regular patterns the trains were then sent on their three to six weeks' journeys with over 2,000 people per train. The routes ended often in the Caucasus, at the Polar Seas, in Siberia or in Turkistan, but mainly in the Urals, Donez and Don areas. About 30% of all evacuees died on these transports. 650.000 Germans from the Eastern provinces were in this fashion deported, of which over 100.000 to 125.000 died in camps before seeing a train. In some towns it was announced that on a day men from 17 to 50 years of age had to report with provisions and two blankets. If, however, nobody arrived, all men were taken. The women and children stood at the roadside and were clubbed with rifle butts if they tried to reach their fathers or husbands. If someone collapsed he or she was shot or often just left to die there.

Large columns of trucks were seen to go east. The women and their children were separated. Terrible scenes occurred. Most women never saw their children again or even heard what had happened to them. A German nurse reported as she worked in Potulice, a children's camp, that around eight hundred children including babies were always in the children's home at Potulice during the period from November 1945 to September 1947. The babies' ward was beautifully done out, because here the Red Cross and other commissions came regularly to inspect. The heating was turned on for these occasions. But as soon as the visit was over everything was turned off again. Between 30 to 50 babies were regularly here, most of whom died of cold and malnutrition. If by any chance someone passed the station at around four in the morning they could hear a noise like sheep, but not of babies. It was pathetic.

The older children were kept in different barracks; they were, until May 1947, allowed to go out only at lunchtime. All day they sat huddled and frightened in their cots. Every child kept a safe distance whenever Dr. Cedrowski, the Chief doctor, was in camp. If women ever dared to ask where their children were the answer was always the same: "Thousands of children have gone through here; we do not know where to".

Many children from eight years old onwards were given to Polish farmers to help clean horses and work on the fields. If the horses turned round sharply, the children would fall into the mire or on to the concrete. Brothers and sisters were not allowed to talk to each other. There was no registration for these little human bundles. If a child was killed for any reason, a replacement was sent to the farmer. They were like anything else, replaceable. The camps were cleaned and the children dressed only when an inspection was imminent. Most of the children were not allowed to speak German. When it came to the repatriation of some of the children to the DDR in 1949, they had forgotten or, as with babies, never learned their own language. From Potulice the children were transported to Schwetz. Here the regime was just as devastating for the youngsters. Everything was de-Germanised. Some of the lucky ones found homes with Polish parents. They were fed well, dressed well, and accepted into the family. It was at a later time that some of those children were allowed to write to their German mothers, if they could be found. Some even saw their mothers, but the difficulty of understanding was tremendous. It also happened that some Polish parents asked for the cost of bringing up the foreign children, which of course the mothers could not pay, so the children had to remain in slavery. Many of the camps trained some children to spy on their friends. It was a very hard time for the little people. Self-help was the order of the day. 1945 saw the largest number of baby deaths. The mothers had their hands tied when giving birth, and the babies were left to starve. Mothers themselves received only cabbage soup and were then sent back to work. Needless to say the death rate here was enormous. 900,000 women and men were transported to Polish concentration camps in 1945. Large mass graves gave evidence of their hard lives there. Not even the ground or earth that covered these graves was owned by the dead. High-handedness, rage and terror against the Polish population shown by their former German adversaries before 1944 gave rise to a desire for revenge on a scale never to be forgotten.

Late 1945.
Very few convoys of refugees from the Eastern provinces reached the Oder, and fewer still crossed it. The majority were overrun by the Eastern storm or even by retreating German troops. The end for most was really murder and fire. The same

treatment the Russians had practised in Katyn and Warsaw they now finally repeated in Pomerania and other Eastern sectors.

It was the most shocking humiliation ever to have been enforced on a civilian population. I wonder if any of the political hierarchy - or, more to the point, the military conglomerate, have ever thought what damage they did to the human mind of the ordinary population. The children learned to walk in rags, to eat, if at all, the left overs of others, often to rummage in bins or rubbish heaps. The women learned never to be themselves as women, to have to do two or three jobs in getting their children out of harm's way. Many women are still today living in horror of what happened to them all those years ago, that is, not only the physical pains they had to endure, but more often the mental scars which were left.

The German spirit had to be broken, but why on earth did the German women and children, mainly girls, have to suffer in paying the bill? Hitlers and Stalins pass, but the nation still exists.

East Pomerania lay now behind the fighting-line and large scale clearance had begun. All the little hide-outs and run-away places were to be found. A few people managed to escape later at the time of the battle for Berlin. Some of these actually reached the West. A stench of rotting flesh hung over the countryside. The snow had given way to all the dead who had so far been buried in it. Dead bodies were floating in the lakes and rivers; in the fields and meadows dead animals were scattered all around. The main fear everywhere, of course, was the start of an epidemic. This fear shared by enemy and friend alike.

East Pomerania had turned into one large work camp. Every woman and man left there now had to plunder the German belongings. Everything moveable was being moved to Russia and Poland. The people themselves were being declared "Freiwild" (free for hunting down). It has been established that from all the provinces east of the Oder and Neisse, Pomerania suffered most in human and financial terms. More than the bombing and fighting, since the Russians systematically burned down whole villages and emptied the whole area afterwards.

The long planned evacuation of the German population started in February 1945. Stalin had tried at the Yalta conference, from the 4th February to the 11th February 1945, to get all the delegates to agree that he could legally transport these people, but he did not really get his way on that item. Therefore on his orders March 1945 turned out to be the high point for the evacuation procedures.

The accumulated hate of all the years was let loose over Pomerania when the Poles marched in after the collapse of the German frontier. The partition of Poland, the evacuation of large parts of the population from the Warthegau, the hunting down of the polish intelligencia, the release of men from the prisoner-of-war camps, the forced evacuation of the Polish civil workers, the merciless fight against the partisans, the blood-thirsty suppression of the Warsaw uprising, the knowledge of the horrors and atrocities carried out in the Warsaw ghettos, all these and the individual sufferings had turned the Polish hearts to stone. The hour of retribution had arrived and the population of the eastern provinces had to pay for it all. Humanitarianism and human rights were completely ignored.

Whatever Stalin's armies had left the Poles now took. That was in human measure and any other properties not much. The Russians had done a good job. The few women, men and children who were now left went into Polish work camps. Only very old men, women and very young children were held back from farm work.

Long before the Treaty of Potsdam, Stalin's marauders were moving everything human and otherwise east. Day and night the fully laden trains rolled on to a now starved and exploited Russian soil. Goods, as under Hitlers' regime, were important as people. His people had no food, but all the hard goods from Germany had to be shipped, transported then unloaded and transported further into Russia. That many Russians suffered under that strain, the cold of winter and lack of nourishment, did not figure in his order.

Long train loads with furniture, bedding, sewing-machines, bicycles, telephones, radios, baths, bath taps, toilets, copper piping and roofing materials went in the same direction into "Mother Russia". Old folk and children had to load the trains. Eventually even these people made sure that most items were ruined on arrival. Sewing-machines never sewed again, clocks stopped for good, and telephones never spoke another word.

The remaining German people had to report every morning and were then grouped into parties to sweep the streets, to wash, to peel potatoes, etc. A vast number of women resigned themselves to take Russian or Polish lovers, at least it gave them food and a roof over their heads and, most of the time, just one man.

The Poles were by now starting to remove all German road signs and shop names. The de-Germanisation was in full swing. The Poles are mainly Catholic; the Russians, however, know no God, but respect the churches and its peoples' beliefs. The Poles were just having God as a house guest, and even then he was Polish first and Catholic second. The Germans were caught in this triangle of the heathens. After the last few years, unbelievably it was "Regina Polanai": Mother God understands only the Polish language".

May and June 1945 saw the return of some refugee convoys overtaken by the Russians. About 150.000 to 180.000 people tried to return to their homelands. Some towns received a German element again, which was, however, soon suppressed by the Poles,

By March 1946 the second evacuation had begun. This time it was our turn. We were marched down the road after being given 15 minutes to pack what we needed. We all had little packages, mostly made from towels so that we could use them again. We had to put on as many clothes as possible. A feather bed would be rolled in a blanket with some food. From the market to the station, one large column of bedraggled and frightened people, were then herded into the goods carriages meant as transport mode for animals. Some benches were around the sides and down the middle, where some time ago the small animals or baby animals had rested. Once we had found places the train was set in motion. We wondered how many people had already been transported in this wagon. There was everywhere a terrific smell of human discharge and dried blood. An old, cold, coal heater stood in the centre taking up precious space. Nails stuck out of the benches, but at least we had seats for now. During the night we stood for a while to let others sit. The train crept along, stopping now and again. Bands of thieves boarded the train and took whatever they could find, including most of our clothes. In the end people with nothing left but their lives had even less, and possible injuries to add to their misery.

At the next station there was a long halt. It was night again and very cold. Our capturers did not bring water or food or let anyone go to the toilets. All these contributed to make people feel even colder, with cold sweat standing some foreheads. The stench in the carriage was unbearable; even the dead were left lying. Wherever there was a hole in the outside wall it was blocked by a nose trying to find some air. After 34 hours we reached Stettin, which is only 70 kilometres from Swidwin. Here we were marched like criminals down the deserted streets towards the harbour. As a family we were all holding hands so no one could be left behind. It was a relatively short march, but for those worn-out bands even that was too much. We had lost some old women and babies on the train, just to be brushed out of the carriage and left and now it carried on. Some older women and men sank to their knees, never to rise again, with a bullet in their neck or beaten to death. On the other hand, at least they stayed on their Pomeranian soil. We were squashed for overnight quarters into either a school or an unused hospital - I can't remember which. We were all deloused, showered, and again deloused. We were cleaner before this procedure, and certainly cleaner than our overseers. For some reason the Poles, with the help of some Germans, seemed to think it was necessary, that we had undergo this horribly smelling procedure. Whatever happens, there are always some people who defect, even if only for self-preservation. Looking back, I realize that the Poles were very dirty when they arrived here; they didn't even know what to do with a flush toilet. According to them it was for drinking or washing one's feet in. Clothes and bodies were all bathed in one bath, or even toilet, at the same time. Hair was not washed; the weather was too cold. These people had also been too long at war.

The school or hospital had very long and dark corridors and only concrete floor. During the night one could hear squeaking, which in later years I heard again and found out that it was rats. Since our clothes had been taken on the train we laid and huddled very close together to keep a little warm. One could hear the stomachs rumbling and gurgling, but we had been deloused, food and drink were not on the priority list. It was a very long night and even more frightening than the night the Russians came first. Nobody knew what was next on order list. Too many stories had been heard during all the occupation period and we were in a way always prepared to accept the next disaster.

Our last march on Pomeranian soil was from this school to the harbour through a devastated Stettin. Here cargo ships awaited us. We walked fairly slim planks on board. Whoever fell into the Oder, fell and was left there. The inside of this large, dark and unpleasant crate looked like the old slave-traders. Everyone got a small piece of board to sleep on. It was the first time I had come across bunk beds and all were happy to escape more cruelty, or so we thought. The sea was very rough, but it was the way to freedom, was it not? Many years later I found out that two large ships which had left just before us had hit mines and sunk. All we saw that night was large fires in the distance over the water. Grandfather, my brother and I stood on deck, because the air below was shocking and made my brother sick. But it was terrible, terrible cold up there.

Some of the ships were torpedoed and no survivors picked up. All along the Baltic coast were mines, and many a ship with refugees, including ships from Gdansk, was sunk. At one time it was called the "Bloody Sea". At six years old you are pretty sturdy and the sea did not affect me or my grandfather. We were allowed on deck where the air was by far more wholesome, although a storm was raging. My brother, Peter, often complained of the high waves, although he is now a Captain in the German Merchant Navy. Most of the family, however, fed the fishes. There was one old doctor on board and he had his hands more than full. No medications and no surgery nor helpers. Nobody trusted anybody and therefore only helped themselves. Cleanliness was also on the "no" list, since fresh and hot water were out of the question. The doctor was at that time 81 years old and he lived to 95, so the Pomeranian newspaper reported years later. Our captain had to steer slightly northwest to avoid the mines and of course the wreckage of the other two ships. Apparently there were only a handful of survivors, mainly strong swimmers and two people holding on to a piece of wood. Fishermen picked those up that night,

On board were people from near and far, refugees that had already seen and felt the occupying might on more than one horrible occasion. Some reported that in their last town they found houses with masses of dead bodies, where the house owner had killed everyone within, to save them from a horrifying end.

Others had seen where German women were strapped naked to Russian tanks and died there. The women were so degraded and debased they did not even scream any more. The whole nation had slid so far down the scale, that some even spat at those poor   females. They were left on the tanks after their deaths and turned white as snow.

Nurses were raped in the beds where wounded soldiers lay. Nurses had to suffer the most outrageous treatment, often while tending Russian or Polish soldiers.

In all the carnage it also happened that a Russian officer shot some of his own men. These soldiers were raping and killing women and girls in broad daylight and in the middle of the street. The screams were heard far away. Another humanitarian officer evacuated a block of flats and put women and children into it under his protection. One can only hope that during the period of occupation in Russia and Poland some of the German officers showed clemency like that.

Often now reports came in where German women had turned informers. They collected as much information as possible and took it to their Russian or Polish lovers. These women were often more hated than the occupiers. They lived through their own actions a fairly comfortable life. Was it fright or was it just self preservation? We shall never know. If any of these "ladies" were caught by their German neighbours, they did not live long. Others stayed in the East after the war. Some because their foreign friends did not let them go and others because they were mortally afraid to go West in case they might meet someone they knew. It was very often a self imposed prison life for those people. A prison they would never escape and a guilt they lived with to their end.

How many days we were at sea I can't remember any more. The distance is not very long, but mines and weather played their part. I do know it was a few, since the sun seemed to rise gloriously over the horizon, hide behind storm clouds, come out again, more than once and brought with it a bitter cold wind.

The air in the lower decks was really stale. The stench of unwashed bodies, sickness and human excrement hung around. To me even today, death smells like that. I never thought that childhood happenings could return to haunt you in later years, but without reasonable explanations to the contrary, I believe that was where my conception of death smell came from. Seagulls swarmed around the ship, but found no food. It is this bird I seem to remember from an earlier age.

Our ship was the first one to reach the West and Lübeck on the 6th April 1946. Freedom was over the horizon, or was it? Freedom was something else by God. The only good thing was that we could sleep without fear, as long as we held on to our belongings.

Back to the present:
The house of our Poles, that is, their flat, is not very far from the market in the oldest and most run down area of the new buildings, in what was formerly Baustraße. First impressions were of a dirty old crate, crooked steps, a most dingy staircase

and the by now familiar smell of cabbage. These blocks of flats were erected after 1946 and are now badly in need of repair. These grey, prison like buildings were built on the site of the old houses, destroyed by bombing or fire. We are told that in this way they were saved from having to dig foundations. In other words they used the dead houses with their cellars as their own foundations. No wonder the houses now seem to be trying to fall down to the right.

This polish family had been in Swidwin in 1945 and had seen us all being marched out. Are we now here to help them? We must be mad!! The flat itself is fairly clean. He and his family are extremely excited that we have come. Coffee is made and cake brought out, also Polish champagne. He has asked Mappen to bring him a fishing rod. He could not get them in Poland, so he wrote. We have seen them, the same sort, for very little money, in the window of one shop here, less than five minutes from his flat. Mappen paid a lot for it in the West, but she seemed to think it was her duty. From all the parcels she has sent over the years nothing is to be seen. All are dressed well. The daughter even in an expensive tracksuit and fashionable trainers. The cabinet in the living room has, as had the one in the monastery, the most exquisite porcelain and crystal. He has known how to acquire things skilfully and as successfully as the rest. But these are spoils of war. They even have a large TV, washing machine, etc. The bathroom, however, is a pigsty. Quite unbelievable how human beings can, in a civilised world, live like that.

The chap does not work, he just keeps strawberry fields. After a few minutes there he gives us an immediate order for very expensive medicine.

We receive two beautifully crocheted tablecloths. We leave one cloth to be embroidered. The wife is supposed to do it. She works nights in a hospital and mornings in a nursery. The poor woman looks as if she could do with a holiday.

The daughter speaks fairly good English. She tells me that a Polish Professor here in town has found and kept so far all the old registry books from the school where my mother, Mappen and Hans were educated. She has actually seen the books. She wants to study medicine. This year she is hoping for an invitation to a family in Cologne. Her brother is at college and studying mining. With father not working this is all quite an achievement, but they don't see it that way. The government pays quite well towards it and scholarships are easy to obtain. Father looks more lazy than ill. His teeth are absolutely rotten. He is very much inclined to kiss Mappen. I am lucky, sitting further away; he makes me feel sick.

Again the weather plays its part. A thunderstorm is coming up and it is already getting quite dark. We look for our driver and say farewell to the Polish family. We receive an invitation to return the next day or next year and then stay for a while. I think that we have already the barriers of human endurance and moral justification, so that I for one do not want to come back.

My head is swimming with all the new, the old and my own memories.

We are late for dinner again, but have not missed much. After dinner we pack, since tomorrow will take us to Gdansk, where neither of us has been before. We find even talking very taxing, since all the newness has to be taken in first and filed in some order. Without Mappen this journey would have been a loss. She at least has good memories while mine are mostly unpleasant. She makes this country come to life for me. I thank her for that. She can tell me things and show me places that I should never have known. However there were some pleasant and memorable parts in my childhood.

When I was two years old I went to visit my grandfather in Swidwin. My mother was at that time having our Peter. My grandmother was by then already very ill and bedridden. She had for some years suffered from schizophrenia and had now reached the stage where she could not be left alone at all. Very often she was strapped to the bed to avoid her hurting herself. I was told of this just now, since it was an illness that could not be discussed even within the family. The neighbourhood was told that she had gone to live with some relative on the coast, while she was hidden away in her room.

To make things worse for the overworked household I caught cold running out of the house, while nobody was watching, with no shoes on or any winter clothes. This then developed into pneumonia. So, my poor aunt and grandfather had me as a patient as well.

As children always find things to do, although adults don't always appreciate it at the time, so did I. If anybody wanted to get anything out of the sideboard the key was always missing. Who would think that this item should not be stored under the sideboard? Our house maid, was not very fond of children and ended up getting the rough side of my grandfather's tongue for hitting me with a dishcloth. Obviously the key was gone again. The relationship, however, never improved between her and me. The key was always brought to light by me, where ever it was hidden and how many tellings-off I received for it.

The old house was a lovely place to hide and play about in. The cellar was deep, the steps dark and twisting, but for children it was fun to explore them, even if it meant being put into the bath afterwards. The coal cellar was unfortunately not the cleanest place to play, but the most fun. The garden had a large collection of fruit trees and nine beehives. My grandfather always saw to them with a big hat and veil, which covered his face and neck, and a big pipe that came through the veil to deter the bees from attacking him. He even spoke to them; all was very peaceful. No one would have thought that we were under siege at that time. We even spun the honey at harvest time,. It was our feast day with fresh honey. But too much of one good thing can put you off for life. Honey today is a complete anti to me, only to be used for cooking.

Since the Russian soldiers were not allowed into our house by the front door, they often tried it out over the fence from the neighbour's garden. It was very funny to see them try to climb the fence in their bulky clothing. The fence was made of thick wood and stone, but over the years had got very slippery. Not only that - they did not do it quietly; everyone in the house was alerted and another attempt went wrong. The Russian command even put barbed wire on top of the fence at one time. The noise was then even more penetrating and hilarious. All these little interludes made the horrible times more endurable, even the adults laughed then, and nobody more than our Russian officer.

In the courtyard at the back was a large barn or outhouse. This had very big double doors and grandfather hung a lovely swing there for me and later for all of us. Needless to say, the swing was never high enough. But fun nevertheless!! In the period of occupation we sometimes found refugees in the barn. Our silver was at that time buried in the compost heap. When it came to the evacuation, most of the goods stayed there. We have no idea if the Poles have ever found the stuff that had all gone into that hiding place. Listening to the refugees, we find that they did the same things with their valuables and hoped that some day they might find them again. At the time they were much more concerned to save their skins.

I can remember that my mother and Mappen argued about a picture. It was an oil painting that some relative had painted, which Mappen wanted to take with her, since she inherited it. But where to put it, food was more important. But small things like that seem at a time of stress to play a large part. It wasn't even a beautiful picture and I have no idea what happened to it.

One of the family jokes, even to this day was and is;" Say Loko..., no Loko..., Lokomo, Lokomotiwe" What a word! It means railway engine, and for a little girl was quite an achievement. Apparently my spoken word as a child was very good, while our Peter said everything wrong or backwards. I think he must have listened to me and heard what a child hears not an adult. But both of us developed quite a sense for the spoken language anyway.

I have often envied my children for the amount of friends they had when they were small. Peter and I never saw anybody besides cousins. Every household was by far more concerned to keep children out of sight in case they were abducted by the occupying forces. In a way we grew older too fast that way. It made us feel closer and in a twisted way far more independent. In later years both of us were to stand more easily on our feet. We have often talked about this and both agree that it did us no harm. It developed something of a sixth sense in us towards each other. But to play with children would have been delightful.

Peter developed mumps shortly after the first wave of occupation happened. His pain however, according to Peter, was at the bottom of the bed and not in himself. He was very poorly and no doctor was to be had, as they were all at the front. Obviously he had not had a grave attack of that illness, since years later he got it again, this time in the West. It did not make any difference, since the doctors, including one of my uncles, were then in overseas prisoner-of-war camps or in the East somewhere. Who wanted to win anyway?!?

Afterthought:

The original Steinstraße is now so broad that in the middle path flowerbeds are arranged very prettily. The old market has been reorganised and is now used for parking. The Hotel "Monopol" at the corner of the market is in its old style and today is the centre of Polish administration. It is a very large hotel where before the war conventions and festivals were held. All of it of course is now in need of paint.

All small old houses around the market were mostly burned out during the first days of the approaching war zone. The rest of them were burned during the fighting, so only their shells had to be pulled down later. From the small market town with individual small houses rose a grey looking multi storied, in a way unfriendly, town.

A very large bone of contention, which also cost many lives, was of course the horrendous roadblocks and ditches dug around the town. Even Russian and Polish tanks had to struggle with most of the blockages. With being so near Reinfeld, Swidwin itself was built up to fortification strength and was therefore fought over more fiercely. Now it is composed of the usual large grey blocks. The town must have cost a fortune to rebuild. If only imagination had had a hand in producing the new Swidwin.

"Mühlenstraße 4", directly next to the town hall, was great-grandfather's house and shop, just before the First World War. The first floor was rented out. The second floor was great grandfather's. The third floor was grandfather's, while the attic was built out and contained five single bedrooms in which the children - Hans, Mappen and my mother - lived. The attic! It was very large, so that the washing could be dried there. The corner, like a buttress, going around and up the side of the house was a fine look-out; often used by the children and later to warn the inhabitants of the house when the militia arrived.

By that time grandfather had already moved into his new house in Dramburger Straße.

Now to the history of Swidwin:
Out of the remains of a burnt-out castle grew a solid house for the "Markgraf". On the long extensive meadows beside it the cows grazed until the German marauders came to settle.

Since 1280 the land has been known as "Schivelbein" and in 1292 it was an established township. The oldest town seal is from 1296, and this could also have been the time of receiving the municipal law. It is all rather confusing here. At first it was a bailiwick administration with an elected council. The area covered 164 "hides", that is 60 to 100 time 164 acres. The mill by the "Kussennowsche Waage" belonged to the town; today it is a paper mill. The first house of God was the chapel "Heiliger Geist" standing in "Hospital Straße". Around the market were the farms with their narrow frontages. A place for the church was reserved at one corner. Two curving streets provided entrance to the town centre. Here rose the Town Hall, from which the four elected mayors governed.

The councillors - from 1319 "Von Wedels" - had recourse to the highest laws and moulded part of their market- and custom finances to them. With these finances they strengthened their powers, built gates and in 1338 erected the "Maria Church". The parson received board and lodging in the castle. Safeguard was guaranteed for the animal-and corn trade of the citizens. They built the castle mill and created peace and order in a time when unrest and pillage were all too familiar. It is a pity that "Hans von Schivelbein", the last of the Wedels, grew poor and had to sell the land to the German "Ritterorden" in 1384. This brought bad times for the town and country. No strong hand held the numerous Leckows, Brokes, Manteufels together to defend the borders intact against Poland. Indeed, the order reinforced the castle, but that brought no income for the population, only drudgery and taxes.

Thereby the corn trade stagnated and very often collapsed leaving the town with no winter provisions, certainly no extras to sell.

By then the population had had enough. They begged the Elector Friedrich II of Brandenburg to take them into his care. This was in 1455 and from that time Schivelbein stayed "Brandenburgisch"; the population was peaceful and proud of their new overlord.

Some of the history is missing now!!! I have looked in many libraries and bookshops, but to no avail.

Once again dread and turbulence overtook the town and land. Fifty years of peace were eroded through billeting, deliverance and war tax. In the time between 8.11.1806 and 3.11.1808 about 51.872 Taler were paid as war reparations. Even that was pressed out of the poor country by an autocrat. Because of weak finances the town was forced to sell country estates. In this way the farmers got their freedom. The town houses went into hereditary tenancy; the outworks of "Nemmin" passed into the hands of "Schulze-Ponart" from Nelep. At the same time the "Steinsche Reform" was begun.

The Schivelbein castle mill ceased to be a banal mill by order of the elected body. Both town banks were amalgamated and Schivelbein elected twenty four new councillors. The first mayor was Konrektor Plieth. It took time and effort by the new council to organise the townspeople into law and order again. With the onset of peace and all the warriors returning from far countries the town walls burst and Schivelbein spread its wings. The area of Acker-,Baum-and Gartenstraße was built and the new town sprang up on the fields of the original land. The Mühlentor (Millgate), because of its beauty and unusual style of architecture, was spared. New life, spiritual as well as economic flourished. The population rose from 1513 on 1811 to 5043 in 1861.

In the relatively small space of time of 50 years the transaction from a farming - industrial culture to that of a very busy trading town was achieved. During this time one of the industries, cloth-making, completely died out. They couldn't compete with the modern clothing factories, which used steam by now to drive their machines. They had the buying and selling facilities only in the surrounding areas of Schivelbein. Here Sheep rearing declined to provide more arable land. Most likely their spirit of enterprise disappeared as well.

By contrast the merchants increased from 4 in 1811 to 26 in 1861; also 44 dealers settled in the town. The figure for cobblers and shoemakers rose from 42 to 70, which was about right for the population increase. The district population rose from 8750 to 14257. The carpenters multiplied from 5 to 25. In addition to the original 8 locksmiths came 8 saddlers. Dressmakers and tailors increased from 11 to 23.

If one considers the spiritual upsurge of the town up to 1891, one has to omit the press. On the 14.4.1866 one Franz von Flatow bought the bookbinding and printing works from Kuehn and took over the editing of the "Schivelbeiner Kreiszeitung", the daily Newspaper which throughout the time of its existence helped to educate the people. The well known bookshop of Puchstein lasted until 1945, when it burned down together with the church tower, and played a large part in the distribution of the newspaper. The progress transferred itself to the trade. A further educational college was founded in 1875 and improved the education of the rising population. The trade clubs held evenings with speakers, including Professor Vitchow in 1872. How much the doctor and his foresight were appreciated was clear on his 60th birthday in 1881, when a commemoration plaque was mounted on his birthplace. All clubs, which were founded before 1891, helped to advance the mind and progress of the community. The "Vaterländische Frauenverein" (Women's Guild) took root here in 1879. A new Sports club in 1876, the Ornithological Club in 1879, the Improvements Club in 1877, The Burger Club for town interests in 1888 and the Cycling Club in 1894.

The state of the house shows at once the mind of its owner and on this principle the good burghers arranged their houses. This was one of the reasons they no longer tolerated the displeasing appearance of their church. 1881 saw a radical improvement; a new organ and the altar picture were bought. The Jewish community built just before that a new synagogue in Neue Straße. The street was enlarged in 1877 from the market to Dramburger Straße.

From 1864 there were three doctors; in 1879 a new health clinic was opened. In 1879 a solicitor came to town and through the justice reorganisation of 1879 Schivelbein had two judges.

Into this harmonious picture of healthy progress came the Städtische Sparkasse. A sign of prosperity was seen when in 1889 interest rates were lowered to 3%. People were content with plenty of work, quite happy with small incomes and satisfied with small ambitions. There were no really rich people in Schivelbein, but, to counter that, also no really poor ones. Obviously a town consists not only of the major streets, but also of all the outlying or even the less populated smaller streets. All were on good and stable foundations, economically, and very clean. The only blot was the railway, which did not present a pleasant picture.

The nearer we come to the present the quicker appears the development of the town. The old gabled houses with wooden frames gave way to more modern shops and business premises with their glass and iron fronts. There were no more one-storied houses and through these taller fronts the whole town gave an impression of constriction and the streets looked narrower. The only real statutory building was the "Steintor" (Stonegate), but how long could this resist the rumble of all the new traffic?

From 1861 to 1891 was only a small increase in the population to 5935. 18%, while the district itself managed 33%. One cannot blame only infectious illnesses for the reduction in growth, although in 1868 about 330 people died, 200 of them on cholera. 1868 was the year for many children to die of scarlet-fever. Since the decline could not really have had any effect till 1891 it is widely believed that the town provided just enough food to keep about 6.000 people, no more.

Although the increase in population stood still it did not mean that progress stopped. Firstly the school, founded in 1540, had for centuries had only two teachers, the rector and co-rector. A private school with one more teacher was then amalgamated with the old Schivelbeiner Stadtschule (Stateschool) and increased to 1023 children and twelve teachers in 1861. 1866 was the time to move the boys' school to new premises near the Steintor. The old school building became the Town Hall, while the Town Hall was demolished to allow more light and air into the middle of the town. Although the request for a grammar school was granted in 1877, an agricultural college was planned instead. 1881 saw the laying of the foundation stone in the Rosengarten. This school was very beneficial for the town and country and a large number of farmers, estate owners and burghers gained here a solid foundation in knowledge and practical affairs.

The Kaiserplatz (Empororsquare), with a square in front was then a park and looked onto the Reform Grammar School, which was formerly an agricultural college. The

Bahnhofsstraße (Station Street) now follows the progress which the other streets have already endured. Shops succeed shops and businesses. New industries have arisen; vinegar and mustard, mills, saw-mills, brick and stone factories. All these require more and more workers. After that the population rose until the First World War to 9.200. All these people wanted to live and breathe freely; so the five-finger development of the town was born. Great plans were still not realised but for that the worsening economic situation was to blame . After all the houses had been supplied with gas and electricity, the sights were turned towards drainage and water supplies, a hygienic necessity for the low-lying inner town. One part of society which is missing today, but was a colourful feature of the town, was the 9.Landwehrregiment, part of the Home Defences, since 1816. The Commander lived in a part of the castle, with its main building reorganised as an ordnance depot. The main tax department arrived in town shortly after the regiment left and made there space for the new arrival.

The most important event of that time was in 1875. The district was split up. The whole of the Feldmark (name for the area around Schivelbein) was divided up and all the farmers moved to the Stadtfeld (Town Field).

New Schivelbein was born. The manor was moved to the Polslepper Weg (a road), the town estate on the Klüthower Straße (an estate street) was rebuilt, and on the Monastery Field grew Neu Wachholzhausen (New estate). The castle farm was split and from its largest part grew Neu Pripslaff (another new estate), an independent estate.

Through this procedure a farming community grew around Schivelbein again, which sold its produce in the town and district. How much the Schivelbeiner population had to rely on them shows in the establishment of the weekly market in 1828.

With the opening of this market began a vast upsurge of business and trade in the town. Trade itself, however, had its difficulties too, since Schivelbein lies away from the through traffic. Between 1846 and 1848 a link road was built from Stargrad to Bad Polzin via Schivelbein. The road, however, was not suitable for all the traffic and a rail link was soon necessary. The railway was inaugurated in 1859 not too far from the town centre, but a new town quarter was soon established.

This part of the history comes from Rector Kortlepel:
From the Pomeranian Newspaper;
"Oil near Schivelbein at a depth of 3930 metres."

In none of the other towns did the Schneidemühler Prospecting Company drill for oil, certainly not to the depth of 3930 metres, as in Schivelbein. At a depth of 2500 metres they found large quantities of stone, calcium and salt. It was not profitable to mine these, since the extraction costs at these levels are far too great. So far there is not much oil, etc to be found. This was already known before the war. Even then the German hierarchy did not think it profitable enough to develop. After the war the Polish government said they had found oil in these places. After six years, however, they gave up drilling; the German assessment had proved to be correct. To try again near Schivelbein was from the beginning a forlorn hope, since at a depth of nearly 4.000 metres there is no oil in East Pomerania. A large deposit of oil was found in the region of Schneidemühle at a depth of 1.800 to 3.100 metres. Until now the costs near Schneidemühle are around 20 million Zloty and profits, so far, elusive.

Thursday 1st May 1985.
We have to get up early today since the bus leaves the hotel at 8.30 am. The breakfast is large as usual, but today we have scrambled egg on top of it. This, however, when everyone is full and finished.

We start out on the transit route to Gdansk. The first little town we pass is Schlawe, now Slawno. The massive tower of St. Mary's Church can be seen in the distance. The countryside around here is very flat. The town was formed in the 14th century on the River Wipper. It was until 28th February 1945, when the Russians marched in, a lively centre for this part of the country. Exceptional are its flat, fat towers. Besides the church there are two more town gates, the Stolper and the Kösliner (both names of towns here). The very heavy and massive brickwork of these three buildings allowed them to survive the war. Not so the small houses in the centre of the town. As in a lot of Eastern German towns, Slawno has seen the same de-Germanisation. The town centre is today empty and untidy. The little houses built in a chess form arrangement are missing. In their place we find now the heavily built, monotonous forms of housing, even near the places of historic value. Today there are 13.000 people living here. Slawno lost its function as chief town of the district in 1975, when it was grouped together with the Stolper Wojewodschaft (Metropolitan area). In its western district are large furniture factories.

From Slawno we take the wider Kösliner - Danziger Road, the old Reichsstraße 2, and our journey goes on via Zitzewitz, the old main ancestral seat of the Pomeranian noblemen. On to Stolp, now Sluspk.

I had hoped to finish the journey without a migraine, but no, my little friend has come with us. The country looks immediately dim, as if you have only one-sided eyesight; it all swims. So, as usual, out come the pills, since we are going to have a long day in front of us and I cannot possible take out my injections.

The country here is a lot flatter than previously, and I thought that was flat, a lot less forest. It also looks as if it is going to rain. We certainly had enough of that so far.

Before the war Slupsk was the agricultural centre of Northeast Pomerania. It was in regular competition with Koszalin over the major government offices, businesses and associations, but Koszalin had been the governmental centre since 1900 and was not letting go easily.

In 1939 Slupsk was the third largest town in Pomerania. Its nickname, Little Paris, let it be known that the people enjoyed life. The town was well known for the garrison of the Blücherhusaren (name of a regiment), a local regiment. The town was founded in 1310 by the Markgraf of Brandenburg. It was from then onwards in the shadow of Koszalin and Stralsund, but grew very fast and subsequently founded the Landkreis Stolp (Metropolitan area), as town and country of Slupsk. In 1939 with 2226 square kilometres and 83.000 inhabitants in its 193 county parishes it was a very large and respectable township. The market town was a free town from 1898, and was therefore Germany's largest borough.

Heinrich von Stehan, the re-Organiser of the Prussian Mail Service, was born in Slupsk. He was also the founder of the World Mail Institution and the first head of the German Post Office - hence the Stepfan Platz, the big square between the imposing mansion and the former Zeek superstore, named after him. 1945 was a time of destruction for the Slupsk inner town, although there was not a great deal of fighting for the city. The Red Army set fire to all the houses in the Old Town except three. This meant that the whole of the market area and the southern part were engulfed in flames. 36% of the whole town with its 1162 houses was destroyed.

The reconstruction of the town was very much in the form of Stargrad, only in a softer form. Thanks to the cultivation of the green areas and the renovation of many older buildings it presents nowadays a friendly picture, especially near the station.

The southern part of the town was rebuilt in more open form. Owing to the destruction of the houses the Holstentor (Holstengate), Gold- and Höhlenstraße, the market is now remarkably large and square. A large cinema was built. The reconstruction of the Maria Church, without its characteristic baroque tower cap, is now finished. The inside is decorated with red garlands and ribbons. These decorations are now to be seen all over Pomerania. The Poles seem to like colour in their churches. From the market you can now see through the old Langestraße up to the white-painted castle. It is nowadays a proper traditional old square with the mill, millgate and the castle church. This is one of the more pleasant towns around here.

The Bahnhofstraße is the main shopping-area with its many shops. With the conversion of the northern carriageway to a pedestrian way we have a very pleasant view all around. The old building style has been kept and the buildings have been repainted in the last few years. The trams were removed years ago. The station was never rebuilt, but a wooden hut was erected for the ticket-office, while the rest of the station is used for only goods and luggage.

Since 1975 Slupsk has been the centre of the Wojewodschafts-Behörden (Government Offices) accommodated in the old Landratsamt (Town Hall). It include the eastern part of the old Slawno, the land of Slupsk itself. The original district of Rummelsburg, Bütow, Schlochau and the western part of Lauenburg. Inhabitants now number around 90.000. On the western side of the railway are huge blocks of flats to house a vast number of people.

* * *

On the night of the 8th to the 9th of March 1945 most of the inner city went up in flames. Many German men were forced at bayonet point to pour petrol into the houses and light the lot. Women and children were apportioned to different lorries; the screams from either were terrible and could be heard from quite some distance away. Of these unhappy beings none was ever seen again. Others were literally tramped to their deaths, since ammunition was too precious to be wasted on Germans. The last train, which left on the 6th of March 1945, full of wounded, did not go west as indicated, but east towards Gdansk. Nothing went west any more at that time.

It was reported from Slupsk that on the first days of the Russian occupation about 4.000 people were buried in mass graves. Since the distillery was just the find for the occupier, the Red Army forces were mostly drunk, and anything and anybody were fair game. Many women and men took their lives and those of their children, so they would not be forced to live through the horrors to come. But this applied not only to Slupsk; it was a way out all over the country. Very often the attempt to take one's life went wrong, since most people tried to cut their wrists and did not go deep enough; so the wounds healed up; but the penalties were much harsher. Here, as in all other towns, the men were separated from their families, often to be lodged in churches until marched for miles to waiting trucks, from there to be taken to railway stations, or even to march all the way to their final destination. Many people never came back; many ended in the Urals, etc.

A report from the 9th July 1945 by a parson from Slupsk stated that the militia was more a bunch of criminals than police. They turned out first thing in the mornings to comb the streets and find out who went for milk, etc. The women who had to leave their children often did not return, or if they did, late at night, to find their house completely empty. Their children were sent to some camp and the other belongings to Poland.

Nobody and nothing was safe.

August 1945 saw mass evacuations from Slupsk, believed to be to the Urals. On route, whenever the trains stopped, new hordes of vandals came on to the trains, or the old band of robbers left. The women and children were the main sufferers once more. When these trains reached any major station many dead or dying were thrown out, mostly naked. Many trains reached their destination with only naked people, everything had been stolen on the way. The cargo itself was more dead than alive.

On and on we go through the sandy ridges of hills towards Lauenburg, now Leborg. Before the town are large patches of forest. Before the war many hunters came to try their hand at catching wild animals. Today, however, the wild ones have to be treated with care, as there are not many of them left. Lots of them were killed during the war and afterwards for food. Limited numbers of West German hunters are again allowed to come and hunt, but in return for a handsome pay-off to the Polish government. Not all the animals killed can be taken home either; the control is very strict. Wild life is under protection, and rightly so.

Leborg was Pomerania's most worth eastern district town. The distance from Szczecin is 275 kilometre, but only 20 kilometre from the pre-war national border, which prohibited the hustle and bustle of our earlier times. Because of the blue shine over its country side, the land was also known as the "Blue Country".

The German order of knights, through their founder Hutger von Emmerich, founded the town in 1341. The plan was in exactly the same form as that of all the other settlements, where the castle stood in one corner of the square. This formation is more a political than a defensive one. The town got the Kulmer Law, which is a further development of the

Magdeburger town law. Leborg got a city wall which had two gates, three corner towers and 29 tower-shaped Wiekhouses. Existing to this day are the Ivy Tower and part of the wall. In 1939 Lauenburg was a busy district town. It received a college for teacher-training in 1933. A third of the town was destroyed in 1945 and in the town centre 59% of the houses were burned down. The reorganisation of Leborg was done in the same style as in many other towns and it lost its character with it. Out of 34 houses around one square, only two remained. By clearing all ruins and not rebuilding, the eastern part of the town centre is much larger now, so that St.Jacob's Church is now visible from the market.

The town was taken from the control of Szczecin in 1945 and given to Gdansk, which was a move the Poles would have liked in 1919. 1975, however, saw the return of the western part to Szczecin.

In Lauenburg in March 1945, many nights were disturbed by the cries and screams of older and younger human voices that were taken by the Russian soldiers. Many females were never seen after that. They had to report for "rabota" (work), but the reports that came back were gruesome

Further on we come to the old military road towards Neustadt, which because of the war and the fighting for Gdansk, was largely destroyed. Troops on both sides were dug in and around the town. The hills gave easy cover and the battle was very long and bitter. Today there are mainly the now familiar housing blocks, fairly pleasant gardens and otherwise very flat land. The wind is much stronger and we feel that we are getting nearer to the waterfront. The old military highway is now the 52. A pity, but there is nothing more to say about Neustadt; either I was inattentive or our group leader had nothing more in his repertoire. On the other hand, however, there was very little left of the town after the war. It is also possible that the guide just waffled his way through an account of all the new installations the Poles had set up. But after reading up afterwards I found what this country had achieved, but forgot to say that the West had sent most of the materials, knowledge and often the labour to fulfil the Polish dream.

I completely forgot that we stopped just after Slupsk near a very little lake, where the smell of mud and the croaking of frogs were overpowering, but it is amazing to think that such a place still exists. As usual we had coffee, cocoa or whatever else we wanted. On leaving the bus we had to put on our coats and jackets, since it was now cold outside, in spite of the sun trying to come through. We do forget that it is only May, but for a journey in the bus it is more pleasant if the sun does not shine too strongly. Many people just do not open windows when travelling, the fear of draughts and the love of fresh air being irreconcilable.

A very pleasing motorway brings us into Gdansk. From a distance it really looks like a City, a vast number of grand houses and reasonably wide streets, like avenues with large trees.

The history of the city goes back to the 6.th century, but more of that later. First to our hotel, which this time is absolutely marvellous!!! NOVOTEL is the pearl, all white and, of course, another Orbis-hotel, as all tourism in Poland is under Orbis and therefore nationalised. The reception is very friendly, even warm. The influence of American-Polish visitors is very remarkable. Our room is very attractively carpeted and also all white decorated. The beds are pure white with red blankets on, which are wonderfully soft. Everything is perfectly clean and smooth. This is paradise after Koszalin. After a short lunch we leave for the Zisterziener Abbey church, which has been a cathedral since 1926. The Gothic main building, with its additional late-romantic parts in the middle, came from the

14th century. We are here to listen to an organ concert.

The organ has indeed a deep and clear sound. It was built by Jan Wulf and Frederyk Dolitz between 1763 and 1793. The Park of Oliwa was the original rose garden. Part of the national museum is now in the 17th. century abbey palace. The concert lasted about an hour, the church being completely packed. This is a memorable feature of any visit to Gdansk. After all the hustle and bustle of the last few days we enjoy a comforting rest in lovely surroundings and fantastic music. After one and a half hours of complete heaven it is back to the three-part-town. We pass the shipyard of Gdansk, with its high monument for the Workers' Revolution. Quite a sight! The tram drives along a lovely, tidy main road to the old town, where we leave the vehicle, since our visit to this part of town starts now and is on foot.

The old town of Gdansk is still preserved in the old styles of Gothic, Renaissance and Baroque as nowhere else in Europe. Here in the old part one can still find artistic miniature works, art-galleries, souvenir shops, etc, with articles made from amber, the treasure of the Baltic, besides many pieces made from wood. It feels as if one is transported into the last century.

We stroll along the Königsweg (Kingsway), through the Golden Gate, built in the 17.th century by architect Jan Strakowski, after a plan by the Flemish architect Abraham von den Block. The building is adorned with a lot of decorative items to mirror the high time of the Dutch Renaissance.

Today, however, the Armoury is a High school for the Arts. On its ground floor is a restaurant. Next to the Armoury now is the New Theatre, even by today's standards a modern, but quite beautiful building. The acoustics are quite remarkable. On the performance list for this term, besides some modern plays, are Goethe, Shakespeare and other old favourites.

Along the Kingsway we find extraordinary patrician houses, whose frontages show all architectural styles. The Mansion of the constitutional city is a brick building from the 14.th century. The tower is 82 meters high and crowned with the statue of King Zygmunt August. The most beautiful is the large Town Hall, also called the Red Hall. Its inner decorations are kept in the original colours of red. At the moment it is occupied by the historic museum. The Lange Markt (Long Market) is a trade and conference centre. On the left-hand side is the Artushof, the most elaborate and oldest of the three still existing courts in Europe. It was built as a house for the traders. The material was brick and the style Gothic with an extraordinary facade from the 17.th century. The gallery for modern arts is temporarily established in the building. In front of the Artushof is the very well known Neptunbrunnen (Neptune's Well). The bronze figurine is a piece of sculpture by Peter Husen from 1615. Neptune has in one hand the dish for receiving the blood of the victim and in the other hand the trident, from whose tines water spurts. Along the way are many richly decorated, very pretentious patrician houses. The Golden House, Nr.41, with its rich sculptures, is one of the most beautiful. A walk through history, it will always be in my memory for its sheer beauty.

The Green Gate now ends the Kingsway. It was built in the 16.th century, very massive and used as the seat for the Polish kings. It was built in the style of the Italian and Dutch Renaissance. Passing through its arcade one reaches the harbour. On the banks of the River Moldau is the famous Krantor, a lovely Gothic Gate with two towers, from the first half of the 15.th century. It possesses a built-in wooden harbour crane also from the 15.th century. Today it houses the Seafarer Museum. The wooden crane is the only one of its type left in Europe. It is a very good example and looks very impressive against its background.

From the Green Gate we carry on to the late Gothic Marienkirche with its 25.000 seats, one of the largest churches in Europe. One finds inside numerous Gothic and late Gothic sculptures, including the one of the "Beautiful Madonna" from 1420. If anything, this church leaves one with the feeling of cold loneliness, perhaps because of its size. Looking around one sees there are a few people sitting in prayer here, including children, but not many. The atmosphere itself is cold and musty.

Before 1939 Gdansk was annexed to Poland, but administered by League of Nations as a Free City, then became Gdansk and East Prussia under the German umbrella, until 1945 it was returned to Polish hands. The city received terrible damage during the last days of fighting. The town centre was almost completely flattened, up to 99% of it burnt out. The Poles rebuilt Gdansk in the old style. The attractive houses today are all new, that is the facades were rebuilt in their original styles; the insides we can't be sure of. Even the cobblestones were re-laid. To look at Gdansk, one comes to the conclusion that there was no war here in 1945.

Many of the local inhabitants were not too pleased to see all the refugees pouring into their city, many from Pomerania. They blamed this poor bedraggled mass for all their troubles, including the whole war. To their way of thinking if Hitler had not taken Gdansk from the Poles they would still be living in peace. So even in a German city these travellers were even then not wanted, that was in 1944. Some twisted minds thought if the Poles returned, peace would also. Unfortunately Gdansk had to be destroyed first. The logic was that they were living far too far away from Berlin to be bothered with war.

Many refugees had been running from the Russian Armies for months. Some came from Königsberg (Karlinengrad); they had been to Pomerania already and when the front closed were shuffled back here. These people had lived through the war and lost everything, often even their self-respect. The good burghers of Gdansk never gave it a thought that the city was for centuries in German hands and only a short time under Polish government.

Gdansk was mentioned even in the 6.th century, but under the name of Dyddanzk and was the seat of the Pomeranian nobility. That is the way we meet the town at the beginning of this century, it was at that time annexed to Pomerania. In the 10th century a Slavic castle was built, whose inhabitants lived by fishing and sea-trading. The German Ritterorder took over the town in 1308 and only after 146 years gave it back to the Poles. Under this umbrella Gdansk was free of trade and became a "Freetown".

The 16th century saw another upsurge in the fortunes of the city. "It had been evangelic" since the Reformation. Because of the collapse of the Hanse and the wars between Poland and Sweden there was a rapid deterioration in the trade figures. They sank to an all-time low. But 1793 saw Gdansk in union with Prussia and the improvement in trade resumed. In 1807 the city felt the three months siege by the French under Napoleon. In 1914 the town was freed from the Prussians and Russians and got its city functions back. In 1827 the Klawitter-wharf was built for merchants ships and in 1891 followed the Schichau-wharf for merchant ships, while the Kaiserliche wharf (1850) was strictly for military ships. All this brought prosperity to the town and its people. Between 1895 and 1897 large parts of the fortifications were dismantled. On the cleared area the new station was erected. In the following years a large part of Gdansk was lost through rebuilding. Only in the Frauengasse (Women-cul-de-sac) were the buildings saved until 1945. The year 1939 saw the town receive its newly formed Reichsgau of Danzig-Westpreussen.

1944.

In less than one year the Russians managed to march from the Crimea on the Black Sea to the Baltic Sea and so turned a beautiful summer into the biggest blood bath. Finland capitulated to the Russians, Greece was cleared of German troops and Romania gave up altogether. The Russians were getting ready to march into Vienna and Budapest. The Kurland Armies (German troops in the northern hemisphere) were surrounded on the northern continent, that is to say in Estonia, Lithuania and Latvia, which were at that time under German occupation. Some of the German troops were later able to retreat only via the sea.

The German lines were still holding in Italy, while on the Western Front the Anglo-American forces were pushing towards Trier and Aachen, hoping to cross the Rhine very soon.

The area in the Ruhr was by now completely devastated; many German cities were under continual bombing. Headquarters of the German forces, however, gave out regularly to all the media that Germany was still the winning side everywhere; mainly because of a general belief that the U-2 rocket, with its tremendous power, had caused very heavy damage on London. The feeling that the British were over the water was quite accepted, but the Russians were coming nearer and nearer and only small, very stretched forces were there to hold them off.

When Memel was overrun and Heydekrug cleared, and in the Elch-lowlands the herds of cows and horses were driven into the swamps to make room for the large columns of refugees, the people still could not see the end coming. It was a horrendous sight to witness the drowning of all the animals with all the noise it caused. That was only the beginning.

Many soldiers, who had seen the Greek campaign and had received the Iron Cross were now wondering "why?" This could only expand into something that was by far too big to handle. Even the air attack over Gumbinnen did not convince the population of East Prussia that they should leave their homesteads. By the time it had all really sunk in, time for fleeing had run out. The Nazi Party had done its job well: even at the last minute, villages and towns were not granted permission to clear out. The front lines had to be held, if only by masses of human beings to buffer the Russian onslaught.

The province of East Prussia was a large grain store: nearly every tenth loaf that was eaten in Germany was produced there. It also housed the stud farm of the Trakehner horses, which were bred between the Memel and the Weichsel.

As in many wars, so here human failure raged. The newly-installed Gauleiters (Area governors) managed to transfer their own possessions often including livestock, to safer zones, but the original natives were not allowed to move out.

The instruction for movements of the Trakehner horses was:" When the Russians get there, let the horses loose to run into combat with the tanks, and so show what they are made of". Just to slow down the Russian progress.

Even when the Red Army stood nearly on the doorstep the command was:" No moving out; that will be punished by death". It was advised to "shoot a few refugees to create order"; or to "boil water and pour it over the advancing Russian masses". To kill a pig was punishable by death. Really all rules of human behaviour were turned on their heads and the animal instinct was let loose

When, however, the people realised that it was now or never, it was in most cases too late to move anywhere. Women and children ran in front of the tanks and farmers and older men, who did not want to leave their animals, were just overrun by the oncoming forces, sometimes even their own forces retreating.

Having to leave your homeland with no foreseeable future is not something humans take kindly to.

Polish and Russian workers helped to load some of the carts and then went themselves with the retreating population. The foreign workers had always been well treated and they saved many a German farmer from a bad end. Often, however, even they were just mown down. It is not so astounding for the Russian Armies to create so much havoc if one thinks of all the hardships and atrocities the German soldiers inflicted on Russian and Polish soil.

According to Stalin, German soil should swim in blood and the population suffer as the Russian peasants had suffered. Many of the refugees were turned back by their own armed forces right into the arms of the Red Army. The population was completely confused and drained of all emotions.

One of Gdansk's burghers reported at a small gathering, that before the war one of their neighbours was a very big shot in the Nazi Party. He met him in town in 1945 and the neighbour was now a Polish supporter. They said hello, etc. and the old neighbour asked in the conversation:" Where are you living now?" The burgher gave him the proper answer and was very surprised when the friendly tone of the old neighbour changed: "Well, then I would advise you not to get undressed at night; it could be possible that we have to throw you into the street in your night shirt. It would be better for you to disappear to the country and that as soon as possible." That from one German to another. This happened frequently all over the country. It was said at one time that the Germans were their own enemy. How right!!!

As in every catastrophe there are always some people who will benefit. In Gdansk it turned out to be some small fishing-boat owners. The proprietors refused to take refugees to the Frische Nehrung (half island in the Bay of Gdansk) if they could not pay RM 1.000,-. The boats rather returned empty. One would hope that these people had to live a long time with their conscience. But then these men had already taken Nazi members to safety. Often for a lot of money. Scruples were not a daily ration for most people; still the ones that gained financially most likely lost lives soon afterwards. It was now January 1945 and Gauleiter and Reichsverteidigungsminister Albert Forster was trying desperately to evacuate the civil population from the area of Gdansk and West Prussia. He was one of the few men still capable of rational thought and a wider vision. He saw the trouble the East was in, but could not for anything in the world convince Hitler and his gang to release the Kurland forces to defend the homeland. He was of Frankish descent and a staunch catholic. He believed in educating and befriending the Poles in order to make and keep peace. He fell out with Himmler and Bormann and promptly had access to Hitler cut off. He was a believer in history. Because of the discord with Hitler and Bormann many of the Gauleiter did not enforce orders and so the evacuation plan was only really successful in Marienwerder. He made contact with Gauleiter Koch, since Forster realised what a vast volume of people would have to be moved if the Red Army put foot on to that piece of German soil, but Koch's answer was: "No Russian soldier will set foot on this secret soil!" Only his religious belief gave him strength to see that the failure of the attempt on Hitler's life was God-ordained. But the fight for time had run out.

Shortly after, Regierungspräsident von Keudell, Forster's adjutant who had joined the 2nd Army, reported that the retreat of this army was unstoppable. He also asked for the evacuation to be enforced. Forster gave orders to that effect.

However, many of the Gauleiters were opposed to it and only Mareinwerder complied. By this time everything came to late and to slow for the civilian population.

A few days after the column of people moved along towards Pomerania the Gauleiter there Schwede-Coburg, threatened to close the borders to East and West Prussia. It was, however, unclear who gave that order. Was he concerned for the Pomeranian population or under instruction from Bormann, to force Forster to give up his evacuation plan?

Forster, however, in a round-about way via Göbbels, caused Schwede-Coburg's plan to be abandoned. One million people, with very few losses, were safely transported westwards.

70 to 80.000 human beings daily crossed the area of Gdansk. A German Army doctor, Dr. Rudolf Jaenecke, reported on the 20th of January 1945: In the lowlands of the Weichsel (Wista) between Elbing (Elbag) and Marienburg (Malborg) the roads were filled with wagons end to end. Only stray German soldiers were taken up; the rest just moved on step by step. Most wagons were open and hastily packed at the last minute. Faces were deadly grim, frightened, and of course, very cold.

The inhabitants of the villages stood still and incredulous in front of their houses to watch the never-ending lines go past. They were indignant when their fences were damaged or front gardens ruined. Most houses were boarded, as a protection against strangers. Evidently they did not believe all these horrors would come upon them, only too soon. The human animal is everywhere the same. Of course there were exceptions where men and women stood along the roadside to give warm milk or other food to the marching children.

Here, as in many cases, the political game was thoroughly played out. Even foreign workers of all countries now fled with their one-time masters. Most of these people had their own nightmares to tell, of raped women and girls, the bestial deaths of men and boys, etc.

The end of the war was gruesome for Gdansk, since its centre was completely destroyed.

The city inland is surrounded by a chain of hills, stretching to the south and west, covered with thick forests. From the top of the hills one can see the city spread out beneath. Needless to say, it could be defended only from these hill ranges. For that reason it needed plenty of men and heavy ammunition, which by this time, towards the end of March 1945, was in very short supply.

All communications with Berlin and the 2nd Army Headquarters were lost, but individual commands of the military police, the SS, were working overtime. Courts martial and their executions took their toll in the last days of fighting. Many a row of German soldiers were hanging from trees and lamp posts with signs around their necks:" I am a coward". But even these shock tactics did not produce ammunition. It was a ludicrous attempt by the German military hierarchy to keep their forces together, if they could not produce any other material to fight with but human masses. It only helped to antagonise the civil population, which was looking to them for help, instead receiving abuse, more no-movement orders and often death to themselves.

In the night of the 26th to 27th of March 1945 the German soldiers and civilians left Gdansk and headed for the district of the Wista delta. The same night the Russians stopped their artillery fire and announced over the public address system:" To the burghers of Gdansk. Give yourselves up. The war is over for you. Your lives and property will be spared." It was given in a pure German voice and apparently sounded very convincing.

Sure, the war for them was over, but that was the only promise kept. The Russian armies settled in as they had done everywhere else. Partisans were shot, most often women; men and children were deported to the East. The town was ransacked and what was left burned down.

Gauleiter Forster, a staunch believer in Hitler, came home from his last visit to Berlin on the 25.th of February 1945 and declared," There are only lies surrounding the Führer. Thank God we have only soldiers and politicians here." He also stated that God (Hitler) had to be defended to the last, but promptly fled himself on the 26th to 27th of March 1945. However, he returned to Hela (Halska), because his conscience bothered him.

A small force that had left Gdansk on the 26.th to 27th March 1945 made a last stand at the old Fort Weichsel. On the 27th of March expolsions burst the dykes of the Wista and formed a great obstacle for the Russian troops. In the forests and dunes a large contingent of tightly-packed refugees and infantry lay. All were hiding between the dug outs and larger batteries. During that time large aircraft formations sprayed the area with bullets and shells and so forced the beleaguered human beings there to draw on their last reserves and march again. Only human remnants were to be found afterwards.

The 4th of April 1945 brought Forster once more into the open. He came in a fishing boat from Hela. Marine officers forced him to see what he had done to the civilian population in not releasing the order to evacuate in time. He was later executed by the Poles. About 40.000 soldiers of the 2nd Army plus the forces from Samland and innumerable civilians were on the 7th of April 1945 transported to Hela. The capitulation was signed on the 9th of April 1945.

In 1948 the Poles started to rebuild the city. The intention was to rebuild the beautiful town as it had been before the war. The reason for this decision was that the Poles had always looked upon Gdansk as wholly theirs. Now they had the chance to keep it, including all the houses and memorials. Today Gdansk is the sea-port of Poland and quite a modern city.

The Westerplatte, a place of national remembrance, commemorates the time of the Second World War. On the 1st of September 1939, the pocket battleship "Schleswig-Holstein" trained its guns on the coastline. For seven days and nights the bitter battle for Gdansk was fought. The town was in ruins and thousands of people had lost their lives and homes, possessions and future.

Not until March 1945 did Gdansk get its freedom; that is to say what the Poles call freedom, since after that the town was Polish. Gdansk is today one of the most beautiful towns in Poland. The tradition of the golden age of trade and industry in the 16th and 18th centuries is supposed to be continued in the modern new Gdansk. It has one of the most modern post-World-War harbours for every large ship and tanker, used for coal transportation or the reloading of all kinds of or for the transit of oil and oil products. The Lenin-Wharf is well known for its workmanship.

The harbour of Gdansk in the north western sector and is called Gdynia. These town parts were formed only in 1922. Even before the War Gdynia was in competition with other harbours around Europe. The harbour installations were nearly all totally destroyed in 1945. The French community helped very much to rebuild the harbour. It has today two dry docks, where ships up to 200.000 tons are built. Besides this, it is Poland's main passenger port with two rail-seaport stations. It is the home base of the "Stephan Batoru" a Polish passenger-liner of beauty. The museum ship "Blyskawica" lies in the harbour at anchor. Excursions to the island of Hela and also into the Bay of Gdansk are possible in carrier boats of the "White Fleet".

Now we are really tired and worn out. We all proceed to the evening meal in our hotel. The meal is quite nice when you think back to Koszalin . Soup, main course and pudding as well as coffee; in other words we are well fed. After all the people have talked of their day it is late again. We have a lovely shower in a clean bathroom with space and hot water. It is a pleasure also to find soft towels. And so to bed. Hurray, we did it!!! What a revelation this city is to most of the ones we have seen before, a modern wonder!

This is now the fifth day.
3rd March 1945.
When General Weiss, in Oliva, heard of the dilemma of the troops and civilian population of Pomerania he tried with all his might and energy to put together a last small fighting-unit to hold the area around Neustadt and Karthaus (Kartuzy). He hoped to be able to withdraw his troops and at the same time evacuate the civil population of Gdansk. It was to be a collecting-point for all German soldiers stranded in Pomerania. He moved immediately south in the direction of Dirchau, turned, and moved towards Karthaus. For a short time a small bridge-head was held to enable people to escape, but where to? Heavy losses in heavy armour and some losses in human lives had had to be sustained. As it turned out, Hela, after heavy fighting, remained the only escape route. The ice breaker "Wolf" picked up survivors north of Schievenhorst on the 6th of March 1945. It was stationed there to search for and pick up Russian boats, but found instead dinghies with German soldiers completely cut off from their units. All this reshuffling of troops and civilians did save lives, so some generals really hoped and believed they could help. The evacuation of Gdansk and its surroundings really ran into trouble a bit further south.

Long and heavy fighting took place in and around Graudenz (Grudziads). The city was made into a fortification and had on the 4th of March 1945 about 45.000 civil population plus 10.000 soldiers from all sorts of units within its walls. When Graudenz capitulated on the 7th of March 1945, only 4.000 human beings in all were left. The rest fought until death, died of their injuries or even took their own lives. Again there was a bloodbath, since a vast number of civilians were included. But the gap was closed and the Russian force under a very positive command moved to Gdansk.

On the 3rd of March 1945, about one and a half million people, excluding the fighting forces, plus about 100.000 wounded from the Kurland, East Prussia and the immediate areas were in Gdansk and Gotenhafen, a small area for all these masses. Every small street, cul-de-sac and alleyway was littered with endless wagon trains.

Horses could not be unhitched and very often died in their harness where they stood. The stench of death and degradation was enormous. The evacuees poured as far as possible into the surrounding houses for shelter, or searched for trains and ships to leave via the Baltic or overland. Food was plentiful, if only the distribution had not broken down. The hierarchy of course had left the stricken siege mainly trusting in the amount of food available, but there was no ammunition left. The SS had been too interested in hanging deserters, to have them unpack the ammunition ships and trains. On the 15th March 1945, the first shells fell on Gotenhafen. There was a continuous growl in the air and more and more people from the north, south and west looked for safety in the over filled camps and houses of the old Hanse city. The ships of the Admiral's East Baltic Fleet took on board whatever they could. Gdansk was lying in the cross-fire of the heavy German cruiser "Prinz Eugen" and the Soviet artillery.

* * *

On the 22nd March the Russians were in Zopot. The communications between Gotenhafen and Gdansk were broken on the 19th of March.

The roads of the town were lined with dead, not frozen bodies any more or humans stranded by exhaustion, but killed in action; wagon trains mown down by aircraft; horses dead in harness; men and women crouched on the seats where they had been struck by grenade splinters. With the last of human effort some 100.000 refugees and wounded were taken out by the Navy on the night of the 25th of March.

Next day the whole town shook from the cannon fire of Russian tanks. On the 26th of March the last ammunition-boats arrived and took back to sea as many people as they could hold. On the 27th March the Russian tanks reached the southern borders of the city. A thick layer of biting, yellow dust lay over every street and house. In the breaks of bombardment the soldiers saw their last hope of pulling together dispirited units, exhausted through lack of sleep and food and short of the vital ingredient ammunition, but it was all so pointless.

Wherever one looked there was devastation of property, of human lives and of animals. People and beasts screamed and looked for help. There just was no more help, even to the point of not being able to kill mercifully. The harbour was now empty, except for flames mirrored in the water. The only life still to be seen was in the area of Oxhoer, where civilians and soldiers tried to find shelter in caves and depressions. Even as late as the 28th of March Hitler declared Oxhoer a fortification, but gave no other support. Small ferries and fishing-boats tried to rescue more people. The Russian forces were soon to cross the Bay of Gdansk. Roskossowski's armies had done their job well. General von Saucken had enough foresight never to pass on to his troops Hitler's defence message for the 30th and 31st of March.

Many of the ships and boats, that had risked their own safety to evacuate people from Gdansk were sunk in the Baltic. Many ran on to mines and met their end at the bottom of the sea. It was not possible for rescue boats to reach them; besides, there were none. It was difficult enough to try to evacuate, but to rescue was an impossibility. The Baltic near Gdansk must have been a graveyard for more than 150.000 people.

Friday 17th of May 1985.
We slept very well and are now preparing ourselves for the coming events. Breakfast is good and plentiful; even the coffee tastes good. Except for having to cut your bread with a fish knife and the Frankfurter sausages arriving in two halves, soft and waving as a limp dishcloth, it is quite a jolly affair. Always to live out of suit-cases is no pleasure, everything eventually becomes wrinkled.

It is 8.30am and the start is made. The sun is shining and the world looks quite friendly. The air is cool and a slight fog covers the horizon.

We are off to the third sector of Gdansk, Zopot. This part of the city lies within a ring of forest, and is bordered by a beach of the most appealing sand. Zopot forms an arm around the Triple-town. It was in older times a Slavic castle, but in the nineteenth century became a sea side resort. The swimming-pool was built in 1823 and a year later the spa hotel. This little town has many visitors, because of its picturesque beauty. It has lovely beaches, the longest pier (512 m) in the world, attractive parks, bed-and-breakfast places, pubs, cafes, bars, dance halls, racecourse and other sports facilities. Every summer they have here a song festival in the largest and most attractive open-air-theatre in Europe. Zopot is today quite a respectable sea-side resort. One could easily spend a summer holiday here and most likely never be bored.

We return towards Stettin on the same route as we came yesterday. Some people are complaining, because there was only a short stop in Zopot, as we had spent too much time in Gdansk itself. There are always some who cannot live without moaning. Since the sun shines many more people are on the roads. Everything looks fresher after the heavy downpour we had during the night.

So, now on the 52 we go back to Neustadt and further on to Sluspk. The rape and other field-crops are now growing more colourful every day. Our lunch is dished up in a very pleasant restaurant, very "folksy". The meal is marvellous with warm soup, meat and vegetables, followed by a plate of ice cream, but of course with the horrible, sweet drink. We all have our tastes and mine is not in this line.

After a good rest we are again on our way towards Slawno, Koszalin, Karlino and at last Szczecin.

Stettin - Pomerania's capital.
First a little history as written by Manfred Vollack in "Erlebtes Preussenland":

The Pomeranian capital grew on the western side of the River Oder (Odra). The river itself flows through a shallow valley 8 km long. Because of its particularly suitable terrain it was from the beginning the ideal spot for the Pomeranian gentry. So they built a fortress, which later grew into a castle. After Christianity was introduced in 1124 to 1128 by Otto von Bamberg, the development of two small villages followed. These combined with the castle quarters in the 13th century to become one community. In 1243 they received the Magdeburger Cityright from Duke Barmin I. After that they were encircled by a town wall and moat.

The town joined the Hanse in the 14th century and with that the cereal trade and fish market grew. Stettin was known as the fish house of the Hanse. For a long time these two trades were the backbone of the town's commerce. In the 13th century a small storage town, the Lastadei, grew up at the right end of the beach. The word Lastadei was created in 1293. This Lastadei was in 1630 taken within the fortress installations. With the demise of the Pomeranian dukes in 1637 Stettin became Swedish. The Groß Kurfürst tried in 1677 to regain the town but failed and the town had to wait until 1720 to belong once more to Prussia.

King Friedrich Wilhelm I enlarged the fortress and made sure there was a lively trade. In this way Stettin was to become Prussia's most valuable harbour and stayed so until 1945. All through history Stettin was slowly growing into the capital of Pomerania. Even the occupation by the French troops in 1806-1813 could not stop its growth. 1845 saw the first enlargement of the town by the inclusion of Neustadt and Silberwiese - not the same Neustadt as that near Gdansk.

When the federal formation of the fortress installations were no longer required, they were demolished in 1873 and luxurious rebuilding took place on the empty areas. In boulevard formation, streets and star like parks recall the French occupation. In place of Fort Leopold, the Hakenstraße, named after Mayor Haken, was built in the early 1900's. Together with the building of the Provincial Insurance, the Stettin Museum and the governmental mansion house made a respectable, and even today, very presentable picture. The years between 1873 and 1914 brought to Stettin the development from a trading-centre, with civil servants and a garrison, to a city in which trade and industry reigned.

The first German Portland cement factory came into being in

1853. Three wharves were built amongst which Vulcan Wharf was the largest European ship builder before the First World War. The paper factory, Feldmühle, was developed, together with the clothing-industry, mainly for men's clothing. The first railway, to Berlin, was opened in 1843; 1899 saw the installation of the free harbour. More harbour installations came and new river regulations were brought into force. After 1938 Stettin is the third largest sea harbour in Germany after Bremen and Hamburg, and by far the largest Baltic harbour. Through the demolition of the fortress formation the number of inhabitants rose fast from 72.018 in 1871 to 210.702 in 1900, and then in 1939 to 271.575. As a result of a political referendum the town was enlarged from 82 to 462 square km. It encircled, therefore the largest water flats, like the Damsche Lake and the forest areas. Through the amalgamation of the two towns of Altdamm and Pöllitz and the 37 villages, the number of its inhabitants was in 1940 over 400.00. So Stettin was at that time nearly as large as Kiel and Lübeck together (428.000). So much for the history of Stettin, a once very splendid city.

Our guide for Stettin is a small but very lively lady. Her German, however, is not too understandable.

Through the destruction caused by the Second World War Stettin's appearance changed dramatically. The change from the German style of building to the Polish had a vast influence in this respect.

First, the old Marienstift Girl's High School is today a Polish elementary school. The old mansion at the Heumarkt (Haymarket), underwent a dramatic change since it is today a museum for the history of Stettin. After it was destroyed in 1677 it was rebuilt. The top part of the south gable received the Baroque style again. The pergolas based on the ground floor were re-opened. The northern side received a composite Gothic style, which was to paint out the original, but not too well documented, facade. In the cellar is today a wine restaurant and night club. Even here one would say the rebuilding has been a tremendous success, if only the filth and muck of the empty district of the old town were not so pronounced.

The Baumbrücke (Treebridge), was blown up in 1945. It was once the last bridge over the Oder before the river flowed into the Baltic. It was rebuilt. Between Lastadei and Königsplatz (King's Square), a very high and large bridge is now at the building stage, with wide carrier-roads over the Oder. It will take some time to finish this project. The Berliner Tor (Berlin Gate) and the Königs Tor, once the Anklemer Tor, and built after the Mühlen Tor, was damaged in 1944-1945. The Poles have since given it three names: Piasten Tor, Königs Tor and the Gate for the Prussian Homage, are a reminder that the Prussian dukes had to pay homage to the Polish king until 1660. This, however, had nothing to do with Stettin and Pomerania; it is just an indication that the Poles cannot separate Pomeranian and Prussian history.

The Hansebrücke - before the war in 1903, Langebrücke - was blown up in April 1945. It was rebuilt in 1958 as a train and swing bridge. Today it is named Langebrücke (Long Bridge). Before 1945 there was a Langebrückestraße (Long Bridge Road), and since 1972 it has been used for trams again.

The Marienstift houses were repaired only as facades towards the Königsplatz. The houses behind are modern establishments. The Marienstift High School for Girls is today known as the Professor-Houses. The Pomeranian District Museum, in old government buildings on the corner of Königsplatz and Luisenstraße escaped the war with only minor damage, and is today a national museum.

The building of Prussian Insurance (Germania-Versicherung)

on the Rossmarkt (Horsemarket) is still standing and is now a training school for nurses and goes under the name "Palais unter dem Globus" (Palais under the Globe). The original ducal riding stable in the smaller Ritterstraße (Knight's Street) are now offices. The St.Jacobi church, a distinct landmark, is now the most important church in Stettin, built in 1187 by the German trader Beringer and then taken over by the Bamberger Michaelscloister as a manse.

This building was not saved. The building of the large hall was begun in the 15th century; remaining from that time are a choir walkway and a twin tower-like facade. 1456 saw the collapse of the south tower and the north tower was later demolished. After that the middle tower was built in 1504. The church could hold 1000 people. In the year 1568 it had 50 altars. From 1530 it was evangelical and became in 1535 the seat of the evangelical ministers and therefore the church of the Bishops. However, in 1677 it was destroyed again, but the Grand Duke had the church rebuilt. Considering that Stettin was Swedish until 1720, this was a generous gesture. This time the inside was decorated in baroque style; the tower was stumped and four corner towers added. After 200 years, in 1895, the pointed tower was again replaced, 119 m high, by far the highest church tower in Pomerania.. In the time between 1820 and 1866 the ballad composer Karl Löwe played the organ in this church. After his death his heart was placed in one of the pillars of the church near the organ, his body being buried in Kiel, Schleswig-Holstein. The Kieler St.Jacobi church contains a memorial to him. The music school in Stettin was named after him. At the time my mother was a pupil here, the director was Mr. Trienes with his wife Hanna. My mother was very much at home here. The Trienes were both Jews, but apparently very good musicians and so escaped Hitler's men. If Jews were useful in their particular trade and knowledge they seemed to be saved from the Nazi anger.

Immediately after the war the choir was rebuilt and a temporary wall was erected between the completely destroyed centre part of the church and the new choir. From 1972 to 1975 a further part was erected and since 1972 the church has been the cathedral for the Catholic diocese of Stettin-Cammin. Owing to the destruction of the baroque furniture, the church today is bare and cold to look at. The existing high altar is the old "Kobatzer Cloisteraltar", kept before the war in the Pomeranian county museum. The once massive tower is also only 55m high now. The Gothic prior's house next to the church was rebuilt; only the gable is in the older style; the rest is modern.

The Jacobi church, which was closed in 1934 because it was deemed unsafe, did not suffer much in the war and is today the church of Johannis combining evangelic and catholic beliefs.

St.Peter's - and St.Paul's Church, the evangelical district church, is today the Church of St.Peter and St.Paul for the Polish Catholic church (separate from Rome).

Now to the once proud residence of the Pomeranian dukes and barons. It has a lively history. The Duke left the castle in 1249 and the town took over responsibility for it. After that in 1346 Duke Barmin III built a bridge house, which was rebuilt and enlarged in 1619 and at long last became the residence once more for the dukes in 1637. 1677 saw the destruction of the stunning renaissance gables. It was rebuilt in 1720 and was for a while the high court for judges. 1944 to 1945 saw destruction once more with the Bogislav building completely ruined. Since 1958 the Poles had been building again on the castle, until it was declared finished in 1983, but only on the outside. Many compromises had to be reached in its reconstruction. Many things from the 18th and 19th centuries are lost altogether. Out of place is the connecting path between the Bogislav building and the middle wing. In the main, the castle won through the restoration. Today it is cultural centre for the Wojewodschaft with its exhibition rooms, castle cafe and concert room, which was formerly the castle church. The building of the new theatre is now under way in the Bogislav building. The Schweitzer-House or Loitzenhaus was rebuilt after extensive war damage and now houses the state-owned Lyceum for Arts. The Seven Mantle Tower, which before the war was just a tower stump on top of a back street house, with a small dwelling on the top of that, is in Junkerstraße (Junker Street). How many could live in such a small place is beyond me. Very unusual! In 1964 it was amalgamated with the town walls with its smaller tower, in keeping with the Pomeranian history design. The present-day Jungfraubastei der sieben Mantel, a defensive installation, is now occupied by the sister office of the Polish Institute for Tourist and Country History. The town library at the Grüne Schanze (Green soil wall) was not damaged in war time and is now Stanislastaszic-Wojewodschafts-and Town library. It houses 800.00 volumes, of which 300.00 were in foreign languages, 30.000 old prints and about 1.600 examples of old maps and 38 Latin printings from the time before 1500 a.d. Most of these were transported to Russia.

The mansion in Magazinstraße (Magazine Street) did not receive any damage and is today Rectoratsbuilding for the Medical Academy. The town theatre on the Königsplatz was destroyed and the ruins removed in 1945. The new theatre is now housed in the Bogislav building in the castle. The Velthusensche or Wolkenhausersche Haus, seat of the Provincial Bank on the corner of Luisenstraße and Kleine Wollwerberstraße (Wool Weaver Street) was rebuilt after the war in its old baroque style, and has been the seat of the Felix-Nowowiejeski-Musical School since 1959 and 1962, when the second part was opened. The water-tower on the Rossmarket with its baroque fountain was preserved in the war and kept its former style. It is now known as the Fountain of the White Eagle. The eagle on the fountain was as a matter of fact originally the Black Eagle of Prussia. It seems eagle is eagle, the colour does not matter. The layout of Szczecin has changed. Before the war Stettin had 400.000 inhabitants and covered 406,9 square km, while it now has 388,322 inhabitants and covers 300 square km.

This is one of Poland's largest towns. Szczecin has taken much longer to reach its pre-war population numbers than Gdansk, since the rebuilding has been much slower. It also reflects the insecurity of the Poles who live on the western side of the Oder.

Since there is still no peace treaty with West Germany, the Poles were only to govern and manage the country. Many of the ordinary Poles fear that they may have to leave one day again, considering that quite a few came in 1944 and 1945 from the now Russian part of Poland. No other town underwent the process of de-Germanising as fast as Szczecin. The Polish Government even at that time were determined never to leave this land again. The Russian government went to the trouble of shipping Poles from the East to this land. About fourteen million people from East and West Prussia, Pomerania and Selicia were evacuated to be resettled in West Germany, mainly in Schleswig-Holstein. Much of the population went to Canada, USA and Australia. The Poles very badly needed the western counties, since they had lost their own eastern lands to Russia. Szczecin has today far more women than men. The men rather work in central Poland or old Silicia where there was and is today heavy industry, including their coal fields.

The harbour is today very busy and moves 900.000 tons a year, while in 1939 only 39.000 passed this port. The warehouses were full of herrings before the war, because Szczecin was the largest collecting-point for these fish. It is therefore no surprise that the Madonna in St.Jacobi Church has three herrings by her side.

Glossary from the Pomeranian dictionary, referring to churches in Pomerania: Stargarder "High" - Kolberger "Wide" - Camminer "Beautiful" - Stettiner "Large" - all are St.Jacobi churches.

This lovely guided tour has been very tiring, since we have left the bus very few times. We are left with very little time to get a good wash and change our clothes. Tonight is the celebration of the last night on Polish soil.

As usual everything goes wrong. We have to wait, because the people before us are eating too slowly. How inconsiderate of them! But it is worth the bother: the meal is very good; even Polish champagne is served. Everyone gets a small souvenir from our Polish guide. For me, of all things, since I do not at this time drink tea at all, a teapot! A teapot for the English Lady! How wrong one can be, since than I have drunk some tea. Mappen gets a lovely jewel box. After that a collection is taken and handed over to him. Some people give their left-over Slotis which are not too welcome. The rest of our Slotis are spent in the little hotel shop. We do not have any bother with our money; we have exchanged well and paid mostly in DM. I slowly come to the conclusion that my head is growing at an alarming rate, to find room for all the things it has taken in.

We arrive in our room, dead tired and completely exhausted. A quick shower and then to bed - lovely!!! This is now the last day on Polish territory; tomorrow is the homeward journey.

Saturday 18th May 1985.
Again we have to get up early, the bus is to leave at 8.00 am. The Hotel Rega is not very far from the border. In just over half an hour we can buy our Krimsekt in the Intershop - two bottles per person - and one bottle of whisky. But at first again there is a delay since some of our passengers are not to be found. We are the last bus to leave and that means we have to wait at the

border crossing. In the Intershop people are behaving like a herd of cattle. Germans always have to push. They will get what they want here anyway, but on other occasions, it is a terrible habit. Patience is a virtue I have learned in England and I find it now irritating in others to push and pull.

As I have said before, the other buses are there before us, but the waiting is not too bad. A small Kombi, which was not allowed to cross into East Germany the day before, is here again. During the time its occupants have been in Poland another stamp for their visa has come into circulation and they had to drive all the way to Warsaw to get the missing stamp. We just hope that we have better luck. The customs people do not find our small amber stones, hidden in pills. After one and a half hours we drive on, everyone taking a deep breath. The DDR-soldiers are still as miserable-looking as on the journey in. Looking on us as returning criminals. Even our money is counted, to see if we have left enough in Poland. In the few days we have been in Poland even the chestnuts have come into blossom and the world looks colourful, if only the cobblestones were not here! Old-world is charming, but very hard on the posterior when you sit a in a bus.

The best comparison to this land is our Lake District, except that it is a larger area and much greener, that is to say clearer. The return route is the same as the outward one. We are going back now on the 158 to Prenslau, the town that was headquarters for Heinrici and his forces in the last few weeks of the war.

22nd of January 1945: Guderian, Chief of the General Staff and his second-in-command were left in his office in Zossen. Guderian, born in the Eastern Counties, would try again to get the Kurland Armies released and the 6th Army under Sepp Dietrich diverted to Pomerania. It seemed the only logical decision if the Eastern Front was to be saved. But the end result was more or less "no". Only very small parts of the Kurland forces were released, because of lack of transport. Until autumn 1944 it would have been possible to re-deploy the Kurland Armies safely.

In Hitler's over taxed brain was the conviction that only Himmler could save Germany. He had a small success in the Rhine area, but Guderian thought that there was no comparison to the east course of events then unravelling . On the 24th of January 1945 Himmler took over the newly-formed Heeresgruppe Weichsel. A man who had no experience of keeping a large fighting force on its feet, he moved very swiftly well behind the lines from Deutsch-Krone to Crössinsee, the Ordensburg near Falkenburg. It was an old crusader castle. Even very small items, like a map of Pomerania and the Whartegau (now under Russian occupation) to mark the oncoming Russian forces, were a rarity. Himmler appeared as a nervous, but interested man, who showed himself energetic. He displayed no mean traits, but also nothing really memorable to his underlings. He completely ignored the fact that the 9th Army was deployed extensively and the Second Army hung together only by threads; but he was going to use them to the full as complete armies. He was in other words spokesman for Hitler. His choice in commanding officers was very poor. The small units he sent to help defend the Oder-Warthe circle came too late since Shukow, the Red Army commander, had already overrun the eastern provinces on the 29th of January 1945 and moved on at a steady pace to Küstrin and Frankfurt an der Oder.

The difference between Himmer's Rhein success in 1944 and his ineffectiveness now in the east was that then he had a full fighting force and plenty of reserves; but now against the whole Russian might, only a worn-out force with no equipment. He had the ability, with his SS troops to create chaos and terror, even in places like Gotenhafen where ammunition was shipped to. Partly through his bad management, the ammunition was not unpacked; harmony in the troops gone and destroyed with the hangings of men, all of which created more chaos. The SS was his priority. His days on the whole never started before eleven or twelve o'clock in the morning. His doctor and masseur were usually more important than his troops. His afternoon sleep was indispensable and the evenings where his own, when he could not be disturbed.

To save Pomerania from the same fate as that of the other eastern provinces it would have been necessary to send the Sixth SS Tank Army to its aid, but Hitler and Jodl (his second-in-command) decided to send this army to Hungary to defend the last Oil installations. Guderian was shocked, but found the battle against a man and his strong followers too much to handle alone. Guderian was to watch, while these bands of marauders sent the country to its grave. Not only was it irresponsible as regards defending Eastern Germany; it was also well known that in Hungary at this time of year the snow melted and a tank army would get bogged down. And they did.

However, it was decided that under the command of Wenck all small units were to be combined and stand against Shukow. Wenck had a car accident and the whole affair fell flat. The offensive was to have taken place on the 15th of February 1945. Shukow's armies were under strong leadership and pushed relentlessly forward, while numerous German units were forced to retreat. Wenck's leadership was sorely missed. The fighting line was now around Jastrow-Neustettin. With the communications to Graudence completely broken it was worse than chaos. Graudence (Gruziadz) was now declared a fortification and was to be held at all costs. Parts of this German army were soon broken and Shukow's armies marched, plundered and killed their way through the surrounding villages. There was no defending of women and children, just mutilation - and death for the lucky ones.

During the German campaign in 1941-1942 in Russia, German soldiers burnt, shot and mutilated the Russian population. Prisoners of that war literally starved to death or were sent by train, in brutally harsh conditions to Germany to work. Many thousands died on the way. The human hate and political wrong doing in decision-making on both sides had been blown up tremendously and the consequences were the hard and dreadful times for the civilian population of both nations.

On the 20th of March 1945 Generaloberst Heinrici suddenly received by phone the news that he was henceforth commander of the Weichsel Armies. He had fought his way through the army and seen with the Fourth Army most sticky situations on the Eastern Front. He was an unpretentious, slightly greying man in his fifties. But experience and hard work had made him energetic and tough. He lived very much in the present time. Above all, he had come through the military school and had learned well the qualities of Prussian honour. He had been very lucky not to have had contact with Hitler so far.

At his takeover, the frontlines reached from the Oder plains to the Neisse (Nysa) lowlands. Heinrici's appointment in effect took the command of the Eastern Front out of Himmler's hands. The whole army had to be newly assembled and assessed, before being amalgamated into a fighting force. The Russian armies had by now established two bridgeheads near Küstrin and Frankfurt. Guderian hoped against all odds that with a new commander these two breaches could be recovered. 600 to 800 Russian tanks lay in that small area and bombarded the country and its people in thunderous continuity. Germany had practically no air force left and not enough artillery to have any real effect. The only chance of success would be in a surprise attack.

It seems clear that the promotion of Heinrici to the high

command was not contested by Himmler. His command over the troops in Pomerania had been nothing but a fiasco. Their mishandling and the falsifying of information had left him in bad odour with Hitler, and Himmler did not like that very much at all. The outcome was that it gave Bormann too much of a free hand. Himmler conveniently faked flu and so retired from army life. On the 22nd March 1945 an unscheduled meeting took place in the yard of the Reichskanzlei between Himmler and Guderian.

Guderain stated his point that it was imperative to cooperate more effectively with the high command on the Eastern Front., so that troops could be released to help stop the Russian advances. Himmler's reaction as usual was rage. It was too early to make that decision. But it was quite unmistakable that Himmler soon after that talked to Hitler, since the come back was quite sharp. Guderian was offered six weeks' holiday. Considering that most of his reliable staff were dead, wounded, relieved of duty or shot for refusing orders, Guderian felt it his duty to stay with his men. Nobody could be asked to take on the battles against Hitler and Jodl, his mouth piece. There were still some generals very loyal to their troops and country, which they saw being devastated by madmen.

Heinrici found on inspection anything but a fighting force. Most of the units came from the Wista Army, scattered in January, intermingled with partly convalescent soldiers, wounded or quite ill men, very young recruits or very old men from the home defence force, customs officers, reserve training troops, who were again very young men from fourteen years onwards, and SS groups from Latvia. Even in that hurried and short inspection it was clear to Heinrici that even now Göhring's air force got double rations when it came to satisfying ammunition requests. But besides that it turned out that they had only enough to kill themselves anyway. Aircraft were very thin on the ground and because of fuel shortages could be flown only on occasions of great urgencies, or when required for reconnaissance or, of course, if requested by any of the hierarchy.

It would have been prudent to accept Guderian's advice and declare peace, but obviously the civil population had not suffered enough through Hitler irresponsibility and from Hitler's men. Heinrici was fully aware that he and his armies had to hold out near Küstrin and Subice or the road to Berlin would be open and free for the Soviets. In hind sight it might have saved many ordinary people their lives. After a stormy disagreement on the 28th of March 1945 between Hitler and Guderian the latter left. He had accused Hitler of wrong decisions, wrong diagnoses of the war, sacrifice of the German people, troops and property, and the disgrace of the German name and culture. Hitler, of course, did not agree and even had answers for everything. With Guderian's departure, all hope for a human and peaceful end to this tragedy went with him. Only Hitler's yes-men were left. He had eliminated the cream of German nobility and German military craftsmen quite categorically and so had nothing to fear from the rest.

On the 6th April 1945 Hitler and his cronies were gathered in the bunker under the Reichskanzlei in Berlin for a council of war. It had to be the bunker, since Berlin was now suffering many bombing raids.

Heinrici made another of his pleas to get equipment, mainly explosives and men with ammunition so that he could at least destroy all bridges over the Oder. It would have been a short lived stop for the Russian tanks and also would have given the refugees a little time to make it nearer the West, but the answer was a "no".

The Gauleiter of Stettin than Schwede-Coburg started hoarding all the food he could find, and concentrating all the men and ammunition he could muster under his authority. He was making sure Stettin would hold out and be defended to the last. Mecklenburg and Brandenburg soon followed his example. It was a fight for supplies and men between the civil administrations. Everyone tried to amass his own forces, but not one really achieved anything properly, since Germany was already bled dry. It only prolonged the agony for the civil population.

Two days into Heinrici's new command he was ordered to Berlin to report on his findings at the front. The new commander tried very hard to withdraw the forces from Frankfurt to save lives. This action was immediately forbidden. It was, according to Hitler's estimate, Oberst Bieler's fault that the forces were in disarray. Oberst Bieler and his troops had fought gallantly for days and weeks on end with no reinforcements in men or ammunition. The chaos within the Hitler camp was getting worse by the hour. Heinrici had reached in a short two days the same cross roads as Guderian before him.

By the 6th of April 1945, Heinrici's hope and trust to be joined by large tank divisions and large troop reserves was not fulfilled. His trust in anyone, bar his own troops, whom he loved, was gone. Hitler sent any troops he could find towards Lausitz and Dresden, so that they could defend Prag. Nobody, apart from Heinrici, took any account of the large Soviet formations around Frankfurt.

Hitler's befuddled mind still told him and everyone else at the council of war that a firm faith, even at this last minute, could and must ensure victory on the Oder. The human price paid by civil population and troops did not matter. Victory was all-important. There had been so many lies in the reporting of the war, that it was impossible to separate truth and fiction. The men in the bunker could and would not believe that the

German soldier had fought enough. Hitler and his group were now and had always been too far away from any front lines to check on any real development. The soldiers saw the devastated state the population was in and the inhuman burden any more fighting would put on them. The charade went so far that the drug - ridden Göhring offered to send 100.000 pilots to the Oder Front. Himmler, not to be left out, offered 25.000 men from the SS-Brigade. Neither man had anything left to offer, but Hitler was delighted. The offers were paper figures, nothing more. But Hitler's mind was so unbalanced that he believed anything his so-called friends and advisors told him. Everyone was eager only to safeguard himself and receive the Führer's approval.

Heinrici left this bunch of play-soldiers as a broken man. He just wanted to be with his troops, to be able to do as much as was possible to relieve their burden. To him it was very clear that Germany was lost and in his own mind he knew that he had contributed towards it, if only by complete obedience to orders. On his way back to Prenslau he noticed large posters proclaiming "The fate of the Bolsheviks will be decided at the Oder" and "He who believes in Hitler, believes in winning this war". What a distortion of reality!

Heinrici could not even persuade the Gauleiters to evacuate the areas behind the Oder. Sometimes they just did not know how to handle all these fleeing people and often it was from fear of facing reality or the firing squad.

The British-American air force daily was destroying hundreds of miles of railway lines and carriages, a mass of civil property and lives. Did these all still matter? It was far more devastating to think that the Eastern Front was advancing over all Germany and not just to the Oder. On the Western Front fighting still continued and the defence grew weaker and thinner every day. Heinrici's only way out was to retreat south of Berlin, but even that was a task, since all the roads were still blocked with refugees. The people were thrown from one place to another, never knowing how long it would be before the Russian tanks would roll over them again.

To top it all Hitler issued an order on the 12th of April 1945 to destroy all life lines in the German countryside, including all bridges, all transport, waterways and water lines, gasoline, electricity supply and communication networks. Heinrici did not enforce this order and promptly received a visit from the Rüstungsminister, Albert Speer (Defenceminister). Speer agreed that it was barbaric to punish the German population even more with this destruction. It took, nevertheless, a good deal of persuasion to get some of the commanders to agree not to destroy anything of vital importance to the survival of the nation as a whole. The officers were still bound in military loyalty to Hitler and often reluctant to disobey him. On the 16th of April 1945 the Russian tanks opened fire over Küstrin and Frankfurt. The terrifying noise lasted until 4 am and then the tanks accompanied by foot soldiers attacked in full force.

Towns, villages, farms and churches stood in flames. Nothing but bombardment, the crackle of fires and human screams were heard for days on end. The "Streetpeople" moved again, but where to now? They were turned back at the borders which were by now occupied by the British and American forces. Freedom from the Eastern Bloc forces was not possible any more and many were stranded and lost forever. Even now it seems impossible that the Western Forces closed ranks against these human leftovers. The American Forces were particularly ruthless. A new wave of suicides and homicide started. Now in 1985 there stands in Prenslau a lovely church with a beautiful gate. There is not much forest in this area. High-rise flats have again taken over the skyline. There are some lovely town walls and moats. It is quite a peaceful looking town basking in the sunshine.

Today many people are sitting in the picnic area and many more cars are on the roads. The first lawns and fields are cut, far too early it seems to me, but obviously the farmers know better than I. I am not a good gardener in any case. At the moment we are passing large fruit orchards. It is more noticeable than on the way here that many more houses have been built since the war and are kept in pretty good condition. Some of the older ones could do with paint, but that state of neglect can also be found in England.

A farm sprinkler, as in Grandfather's time, is in operation. The field is not very large, maybe the farmers here are sometimes lazy. This monstrosity is even on wheels. Many small aeroplanes are used for crop spraying, they buzz around the places like bees. It makes the sky look quite lovely.

The houses in Bedelow are looking fine and even a new one is peeping through. The one feature really missing here is the trees. The Poles did seem to have more trees and the roads looked very beautiful because of them, especially since the land is so flat around here. We are all left with that impression. The Poles seemed to wash their trees. They looked so much greener. Imagination is sometimes a good thing. On our left now is a large Stud Farm. The ponies are playing very happily in the fields. Here again the hay is cut and bundled. Ponies at play somehow look ungainly and yet still graceful. A camera could not catch the happy times these horses have.

We have now reached the stretch of road where the Peace riders with their bicycles are to ride from Moscow to Berlin and after that to their final goal, Szczecin. En-route are collecting points for other riders to join in or branch off in the biggest cycle race ever.

Near Colpin are again quite a few new homes, indicating that people are using their skills and resources to the best. On top of the lampposts and on chimneys are our friends the storks. What a wonderful sight.

Just near Spamholz is a new bungalow estate, very impressive. The houses in the DDR are kept more up to date and in brighter colours. All the vegetable gardens have their little chalets, quite an impressive sight. Like a miniature township. Even a field with cornflowers and poppies has room and courage to peep through. Now here is an address; Death Village! Who would want that on their envelope? All the farms and farming people are looking much more prosperous than in Poland, but it seems they work on their lands much more. One gets the impression that the land is turned over and planted more lavishly.

The new innovation for moving house appears in front of us. Everything that one could think of plus the kitchen sink is packed on top of one car roof. The packages on top are bigger than the car itself. God knows about the weight. The wheels look as if they are begging for mercy. Also let us hope that he doesn't run into any kind of storm or he could have a beautiful flying experience instead of his drive. Speaking of which, I fear the lovely weather is going to abandon us after all, it is getting rather dark in front of us.

Everyone is happy. We have reached Rostock and we can stretch our legs, use the toilets and have a drink. On the horizon just over Rostock a lovely church tower overlooks the town. It seems to dominate the town completely. The harbour is full, but with the same ships as last week. They are still loading, does it always go this slowly? Our driver reports this has been one of the shortest times he has waited at the border, one and a half hours instead of three. It seems that whichever way you cross the Easter borders are a hurdle.

* * *

Reflections on the visit from fellow travellers:

Most people reported that the hotel "Jalta" had changed. The services and the rooms were much worse, but the food was better. That is really a contradiction in terms, what must it have been like before? The Poles seem to be more demoralised nowadays. Instead of working harder and producing more on the farms, they go into the towns. Here they hope to find the streets paved in gold. The population thinks now to work harder is a waste of time, since with more money they cannot buy any more goods anyway. We observed this to be true. The shops are nearly empty of goods, and what remains is inferior. The Intershops are only for those with connections and even then the goods are rarely to be found. The Poles have developed the attitude that the rest of the world owes them not only a living, but also a massive hand out. They literally expect it. We were actually told to send goods, not asked politely.

Our journey is nearly behind us now, the next big step being Lübeck. Through Wismar we are quickly on our way to the border again. Here in no-mans-land one is still forced to obey the rules. The inhabitants can not get permission to move house. They seem to be classed as a different race, and that between two Germanies.

We are faced with the same waiting time at Selmsdorf as on the way into the DDR. Even the boot of our bus is unpacked. Last week one of the buses passing through here had an illegal passenger in the boot. It was small wonder that the passengers of that bus were only released after a few days. After two hours search our journey continues towards Lübeck, the city that many years ago did not receive us with open arms, but nevertheless gave us shelter in 1946.

In that year, after the degradation of the filter camps and the underhand treatment of the Red Cross assistants, we were ferried to our new housing in the West, an old bunker, originally an air-raid shelter. Needless to say, it had enormous walls, and very little windows, more like shooting-holes in a fortress tower. Nobody ever thought of sanitation arrangements either. The toilets were outside over the back and extremely primitive, just a plank over a hole. The gangways smelled forever of human excrement. The bunker itself had three stories. We were on the middle floor with stone benches all the way round otherwise concrete flooring. It was cold and damp and within easy reach of rats and mice. We were issued with mattresses, left from some other convoy of refugees; this presented an easy way to catch diseases. It was better not to use them, so we slept on our packs and in our clothes on the floor.

My grandfather was always on the look out for food or clothing or anything else that was of value. He came across a large school one day and promptly went in. He always said it was the smell of the school environment that pulled him, having been a headmaster himself before. This headmaster was very sympathetic to our plight. After a while of talking and a cup of coffee he offered my grandfather some mattresses, which were left from his children, when they went on summer holidays. We jumped for joy. The floors in the bunker were very cold and uncomfortable, so that these mattresses were a welcome addition, but always someone had to be there to watch that they were not stolen.

Tables and chairs did not exist there. It was just as well that we children went during the day to, at first a kindergarten and later, school. The nights were gruesome. Whoever collected us from the kindergarten often received some left overs to eat there and sometimes to take bits back to the bunker. The Red Cross was no help at all. We were really looking like Orphan Annie, and were treated like her.

After the bunker we went into the camp of Finkenstraße, which does not exist any more. From there we had to attend the kindergarten, which was in the middle of town, over half - an hour's walk away. At the kindergarten they kept a very nasty peacock, which injured many a child or adult. But on the whole I have only pleasant memories of the ladies at the place. After a fairly short time they made sure that we received shoes and some clothing.

From the kindergarten I went to the DOM - first school. Our way to school took us daily through the parks near the Trave, the local river. In peace time this area must have been beautiful with all the botanic colours. Many a day one could find dog's and cat's fur, where people had killed the animals for food. It was good meat for the table. Often police were patrolling the paths when someone had been murdered again. It was a shocking time.

The river divided the city and left us on the northern sector. The connection was a small footbridge, narrow and rocky. But the way around meant 45 minutes to walk or take busses or trams which cost money. On one side of the Trave were some hillocks. From here it was beautifully to sledge down in winter. Often to end in the frozen waters and get thoroughly wet. We had tracksuits for winter wear and, oh boy, when they were wet they were wet. You got home and received a clip behind the ears or a hiding on your posterior, which you promptly forgot until the next slip into disgrace. We did not have far to walk with our wet clothes, but it always seemed endless.

In summer, that area was absolutely marvellous for swimming and games. It smelled of fresh greens and all year round all the colours of nature appeared. We distracted many a courting couple, since it was our playground and not their meeting point. Both sides were mostly cross about the intrusion.

The little bridge over the Trave was swept away one spring by the force of the water and the river had to be crossed by small boats. Of course that was fun! Also quite amazing how fierce our low, calm river turned out to be. The two men that were guiding the boats across were older and had fun in frightening some of us often, when they rocked the boat too much. After that we moved to the newly opened Holsten-Middle School and a year later back, but this time to the Grammar School of the DOM. Shortly after that we moved to Offenburg in Baden. Shortly not quite true, it took two years, before we got permission to move there. All in all we spent four years in Lübeck, since they were the formative years; but we survived and have today fond memories. Going to the cinema had to be the furthest away, since my mother would not allow us to go to the pictures. We knew how to deal on the black market near the Puppenbrücke and received many a cigarette or sweet for looking downtrodden. Also many a chase from the police or dealers, since we were too young to be seen in this area. All that, as grave as it was, made often for an amusing day. Twisted or not we lived quite happily and with a clear conscience through it all, only to shock my mother sometimes when we brought goods that were not openly bought. Most of the dealers were really generous.

It is a beautiful city. The Hanse-City Lübeck, with the largest Baltic harbour of the Federal Republic of Germany, nestles against the River Trave. It lies 16 metres above the water level, has an area of 202,4 square metres and about 224.000 inhabitants. The forerunner of this city was a township called "Luibici" at the confluence of the Schwartau and the Trave, destroyed in the year 1138. Count Adolf II of Schaumburg built on the triangle a trading-village, between the Wakenitz and the Trave, to increase the trade with the eastern Baltic countries. That was in 1143, but 1157 saw the destruction through fire of the hamlet. However, in 1159 a new settlement was established by Heinrich der Löwe for the same purpose. He also gave the settlement his protection and shortly after that the right to be called a town, with new rules for law and order. Kaiser Friedrich II conferred the freedom of the country on the town in 1226. In the fourteenth century Lübeck was the leading power in the Hanse and in 1630 the last meeting of the Hanse cities was held. From then on Hamburg, Bremen and Lübeck, later on Bremerhaven also, were the only cities to keep the name Hanse in their logo.

Lübeck had in its history, which includes many wars, many golden ages. These times gave rise to many beautiful buildings, both civic and ecclesiastical., trading-houses and institutions, many of which are still in existence today. In many parts of the old city one feels transported into earlier days.

Through the extension of the laws of Hamburg in 1937, Lübeck's freedom was lost. The city was amalgamated into the province of Schleswig-Holstein. Palm Sunday 1942 saw the first bombers over German soil and one fifth of the old town of Lübeck was at that time destroyed. At the end of the war the city had taken in 90.000 refugees. The border with the former DDR ran along the eastern city boundaries. Lübeck had therefore the dubious honour of being the only city along that turbulent border.

The Senate, the burghers and various institutions worked very hard after the war to rebuild their city. So the towers of the churches, which were reduced to ruins in that night of bombing, arose again. The city thus regained its famous silhouette of seven towers, which can be seen from afar. This picture gives many a traveller a feeling of coming home.

The development of Lübeck was mainly due to trade and shipping; also many other facilities for industrial products and manufacturing were developed. Lübeck is known world-wide for its marzipan and red wine. Lübecker Marzipan can be bought at Niederecker's, now a large and beautiful restaurant and shop. In our time it was a small shop with only a back room for its restaurant. But the coffee and cakes were always excellent. A place we frequented only for very important occasions, like a birthday. My brother and I had to be on our very best behaviour and mother could for once be proud of her two rebels.

Because the ferry trade to the Scandinavian countries was much enlarged after the war, Lübeck is now often called the Gateway to the North.

It is a very beautiful and old city. The Trave has lovely foot-paths, the old streets are still covered with cobblestones, not agreeable to walk on, but restful to the eyes, especially when the streets are also lined with all their old patrician houses with their wooden gables. The DOM (Cathedral) is today again a magnificent piece of architecture and a must for the sight-seer. So also are the Holsten Tor (a Gate), which stands very lop sided, like the Leaning Tower of Pisa, the Puppenbrücke (Dolls Bridge); with all its doll like figures on the corners, the salt houses, and many more. The salt houses are all along one side of the river and in younger years now converted into living accommodations.

To spend time in Lübeck is a constant pleasure, since this old historic city has so much to show to its visitors. We are entering the town from the Schlutup direction along the wide roads with their excellent villas. In the background stands the Lauerhof, a very large prison. In the Huckstraße, ion the right side, the city park stretches to the Travemünder Allee, along this old street on the left is the Burg Theater (Castle Theatre), a cinema, which we as children and in our teens often visited with pleasure, mainly because it was far away from the Finkenstraße and so far away from observation. Now we continue through the Burg Tor (Gate), along Grosse Burgstraße, Koberg, Breite Straße and Beckergrube past the Holsten Tor to the bus terminal. All these roads we walked as youngsters are now beautifully clean and largely restored. It is a most gorgeous afternoon and all the Lübeckers seem to be in town.

Beckergrube and Breite Straße were after the war part of the black market areas. When the British arrived we children managed to acquire chocolates and cigarettes from the troops. With these goods one could by buying or exchanging get food or food coupons, clothing or whatever was needed. Again my mother was flabbergasted more than once. My grandfather, when he visited us, was highly delighted that we had found a way to obtaining food more easily.

The end of our journey is reached. Somehow it does not seem like a whole week now. We all say our good byes and return to our hotels. My car is still waiting in the garage for me. After a well-earned rest and change of clothing, we stroll over the Puppenbrücke in search of a comfortable evening meal, not such s tremendous task, as along the Trave there are rows and rows of little pubs and restaurants.

It has been a week full of memories, some good some not so good, and all waiting to be filed.

This little verse says everything one would wish to express after a week's travel into the past:

> There is little room
> between the time we are young
> and the time we are old.

I had always hoped to get to the place where I was born, but with my British passport this was not possible for a long time. A foreign passport and a now Polish birthplace did not fit quite well together.

If it had not been for the presence of my aunt, this journey would have been not a complete waste of time, but virtually worthless. My own memories were mainly bad and sometimes inaccurate. I was, at the time we were recalling a small child and everything seemed super large then, paradoxically a beautiful experience, but socially, a step back in history. In a certain way one could feel sorry for the people living there, but they wanted it that way. If German settlers had stayed and worked with the Polish population, the land would have been developed and more could have been produced in the towns, with a consequent improvement in the social conditions of the whole country.

There is now a new move in Germany whereby German farmers can apply to go to Poland and farm the land and make it their home. Everything seems to work in reverse. The new farmers get help with their settlement from both governments. The Poles themselves are not very motivated, since their own government does not seem to care for its people very much.

It has been nevertheless, a journey I would not have missed. It did not strike me as a "Fatherland" any more and a settlement there for me in these conditions or even others would be out of the question. For success in such a move we have been away too long and seen much happier times and places.

Excerpts from the books:
Pommern 1951, cuttings from the Pommernzeitung 1952
Erlebtes Preussenland, "die Pommern", "Pommernbook"
H.E. Jahn in Pommersche Passion
J.Thorwald: Es begann an der Weichsel - das Ende an der Oder

37857490R00099

Printed in Poland
by Amazon Fulfillment
Poland Sp. z o.o., Wrocław